# Cooking with Amore

## 100 Vegan Recipes for health, well-being and spiritual evolution

MARIA AMORE

AuthorHouse™ LLC
1663 Liberty Drive
Bloomington, IN 47403
www.authorhouse.com
Phone: 1-800-839-8640

© 2014 Maria Amore. All rights reserved.

No part of this book may be reproduced, stored in a retrieval system,
or transmitted by any means without the written permission of the author.

Published by AuthorHouse 04/16/2014

ISBN: 978-1-4918-1390-4 (sc)
ISBN: 978-1-4918-7007-5 (e)

Library of Congress Control Number: 2014904344

Any people depicted in stock imagery provided by Thinkstock are models,
and such images are being used for illustrative purposes only.
Certain stock imagery © Thinkstock.

This book is printed on acid-free paper.

Because of the dynamic nature of the Internet, any web addresses or links contained in this book may have changed since publication and may no longer be valid. The views expressed in this work are solely those of the author and do not necessarily reflect the views of the publisher, and the publisher hereby disclaims any responsibility for them.

# *Cooking With Amore*

*100 Vegan Recipes for Health,
Well-Being and Spiritual Evolution*

Maria Amore

FOR THE ANIMALS

# Praise for *Cooking with Amore*!

*Maria puts so much love and thought into all her recipes! She never disappoints when it comes to taste, and the types of ingredients she selects are always with your best health in mind. Some of my Amore favorites include her chocolate pudding, la Mexicana cilantro salad, and the almond arugula pesto (which is so versatile and yummy). Thanks for inspiring me to eat more consciously!*
**~Olivia Deane**

*I tried the vegan lasagna rolls. I'm very impressed that my Italian roots can be brought to vegan form without skipping in taste. Maria has taken the whole industry to a new level without taking away taste, but rather adding more flavor and a healthy green approach. Cooking with Amore is a book that will inspire vegans and non-vegans alike.*
**~Gabriella Luciano**

*Maria's cooking never ceases to surprise and amaze me. Vegan food without compromise! This book should be on everyone's kitchen counter: meat eaters, vegans and everyone in between!*
**~Ron Harris**

*I made Maria's vegan meatloaf and it was delicious! I am not even a vegan; however, I am slowly learning to eat healthier and made changes to my diet due to Maria's inspiration. I always look forward to the information she offers on better eating and the different recipes she shares with us every day on Facebook. Thank you, Maria, for encouraging so many people to eat better one day at a time!*
**~Dominique Pirolo**

*Maria has touched many people with her love and inspiration. But it doesn't stop there. I have paid it forward. I've inspired friends and family members to live and eat healthier and to be more aware of the pain and suffering of animals. Change may be slow, but it's definitely happening. Thank you, Maria, for YOU!*
**~Joe Albanese**

*I've tasted and tried quite a few recipes from* Cooking with Amore. *Not only are they delicious, but also good for you, good for the environment and, more importantly, good for the animals! A plant-based diet is the way of the future and Maria in all her wisdom has understood that. She demonstrates it with love ("Amore") on every page! Your taste buds won't disappoint you with her wonderful recipes.*
**~Alexandra Sidarous**

*I had the chance to take a cooking class with Maria Amore. The dishes were simple, tasty, healthy and delicious. I'm really looking forward to trying her new recipes!*
**~Maria Grassagliata**

*Tasting Maria's dishes makes me so proud to be vegan. I've enjoyed everything she's made and admire her skill and dedication in preparing so many delicious recipes.*
**~Marc-Joseph Chalfoun**

*Maria: you are our inspiration with all these beautiful vegan recipes! We love and treasure you!*
*~Pina Ciccarelli*

*Saving the planet and our health one recipe at a time, Maria never fails in converting traditional meals into vegan masterpieces. Every colour, every texture and essence, it's like an exact science for her, in perfect equilibrium. It is no wonder that I feel energized and inspired with every scrumptious bite. Share Maria's vision by preparing one of her delectable recipes. Yes even you non-vegans! Warning: you just might fall in love with Maria's recipes!*
*~Felicia Amore*

*Being Maria's mom allows me to witness many of her divinely inspired creations. The delicious success of every recipe is the result of all the love she channels into the food she prepares. You can literally see her doing this if you watch her cook! Spices tingle, flavors mingle, sweetness melts and aromas intoxicate!*
*~Lina Zacchia*

*Maria's cooking cultivates a love for both savoring food and preparing it. Her dishes invite your palate to dive into a world of multi-faceted texture and pleasure, leaving you feeling satisfied and at the same time eager to discover more. Vegan or not,* Cooking with Amore *is just that - a vehicle for love: love of sensory ecstasy, infinite nourishment and nature's healing abilities.*
*~Kim Mecca*

*Maria's cooking is absolutely addictive and excites the palate to the point where one may feel as though they are experiencing food for the first time. Her recipes are so good they can convert any meat eater if they dare to hang around Amore's kitchen long enough.*
*~Santino Coco*

"A human being is a part of the whole called by us universe, a part limited in time and space. He experiences himself, his thoughts and feeling as something separated from the rest, a kind of optical delusion of his consciousness. This delusion is a kind of prison for us, restricting us to our personal desires and to affection for a few persons nearest to us. Our task must be to free ourselves from this prison by widening our circle of compassion to embrace all living creatures and the whole of nature in its beauty."
~Albert Einstein

*Go within; reconnect to your heart.*
*Meet your soul; feel your own infinity and eternal nature.*
*Evolve into compassion for all beings.*
*Feel our Connectedness: We are One.*

# Contents

**Acknowledgements** ............................................................................. 10

**Preface** ............................................................................................... 13

**Tips from Amore's Kitchen** ................................................................ 15

**Soups** ................................................................................................. 18
1. Mega Protein Bowl: Kale and Bean Stew ................................... 19
2. Autumn Harvest Bowl: Three Squash Soup ............................... 20
3. Bonnya's Potato and Garlic Soup ............................................... 21
4. Rapini Lentil Stew ....................................................................... 22
5. The Market Soup: Quinoa-Cream of Leek ................................. 23
6. The Bucerias: Avocado Soup ..................................................... 24
7. The India: Quinoa-Cream of Carrot ............................................ 25
8. A Vegan's Italian Minestrone ...................................................... 26
9. Split Pea Soup with Smoked Kale .............................................. 28
10. Quinoa-Cream of Broccoli .......................................................... 29
11. Lina's Vegetable Broth ............................................................... 30

**Salads, Dips and Pâtés** ..................................................................... 31
1. The Mayan: Tomato Cacao Salad ............................................... 32
2. Bean and Celery Salad ............................................................... 33
3. Cheeky Chickpea Salad ............................................................. 34
4. Almond Arugula Pesto ................................................................ 35
5. Classic Italian Potato Salad ........................................................ 36
6. The Sensualist: Roasted Eggplant and Pepper Delicacy ........... 37
7. A Vegan's Caesar Salad ............................................................. 38
8. Amore Veggie and Seed Pâté .................................................... 40
9. String Bean Moroccan Olive Feast ............................................. 41
10. Maria's Heavenly Hummus ......................................................... 42
11. Quinoa Chia Crunch Salad ......................................................... 43
12. Kim's Asian Flavors Cabbage Salad .......................................... 44
13. Health-Kick Beet Salad ............................................................... 45
14. The Josephine: A Tahini Dressing .............................................. 46
15. La Mexicana: Cilantro Salad ....................................................... 47
16. Yin-Yang Counterbalance: Mango Avocado Salad .................... 48
17. Two Coleslaws: Spicy Italian and Creamy Classic ..................... 49

18. Lemon Lime Bean Medley Salad .................................................................................... 50
19. Creamy Cashew Onion Dip ........................................................................................... 51
20. Kale Goji Berry "Rocket Fuel" Salad .............................................................................. 52
21. Basil Artichoke Spread .................................................................................................. 53
22. Baba Maria Ganoush ..................................................................................................... 54
23. Maria's Guacamole ........................................................................................................ 55
24. Arabian Mint Lentil Salad .............................................................................................. 56
25. El Tabbouleh Loco ......................................................................................................... 57
26. A Taste of Autumn Salad .............................................................................................. 58
27. Parma-Sprinkled Bruschetta ........................................................................................ 59
28. Immune-Boosting Raw Garnish ................................................................................... 60

## Fully Plant-Based Main Meals and Side Dishes .................................................................. 61
1. A Vegan's Shepherd's Pie with Cashew-Creamed Corn ............................................. 62
2. Tofu Mex Scramble ....................................................................................................... 64
3. Felicia's Eggplant No-Parmigiana ................................................................................. 65
4. Rapini Mushroom Black Bean Pilaf .............................................................................. 66
5. Brown Basmati and Long Grain Wild Rice with Green Veggies ................................. 67
6. Moroccan Flair Vegan Poutine ..................................................................................... 68
7. "For The Love of Chickens" Casserole with Cashew-Creamy Mushroom Sauce ..... 70
8. Roasted Red Pepper and Eggplant Risotto ................................................................. 74
9. Lasagna Rolls with Tofu Ricotta and Basil Tomato Sauce .......................................... 75
10. Lina's Polpette: No-Meatballs ...................................................................................... 77
11. Green Vegetable Sesame Risotto ................................................................................ 79
12. Collard BLT Wraps with Tempeh Bacon ...................................................................... 81
13. Amore's Chili Sin Carne ................................................................................................ 83
14. Veggie Lover's Casserole ............................................................................................. 85
15. Maria's Beany-Creamy Christmas Lasagna ................................................................ 87
16. Moroccan Stuffed Zucchini .......................................................................................... 89
17. Portobello Burger .......................................................................................................... 90
18. Sweet Potato Fries ........................................................................................................ 91
19. Bunless Tempeh Burger ............................................................................................... 92
20. The Pasqualina: Kalamata Olive Pesto with Sautéed Kale and Sundried Tomatoes ......... 93
21. Lentil No-Meatloaf ........................................................................................................ 94
22. Spring-Tasting Spring Rolls ......................................................................................... 96
23. Mung Bean Quinoa Pilaf ............................................................................................... 98
24. Splendid Spelt Gnocchi ................................................................................................ 99
25. Pizza Vegana ............................................................................................................... 101
26. Curried Chickpeas with Couscous ............................................................................. 102

27. Carnaval Tacos Veganos with Mexican Bean and Corn Salad .................................................. 103
28. Pasta e Fagioli with Homemade Tagliatelle................................................................................ 105
29. Sweet Potato Veggie Bean Cotoletta with Iceberg Lemon Salad ......................................... 107
30. Maria's Summer Fiesta Pasta Salad ........................................................................................... 109
31. Tandori Tempeh with Spiced Sweet Potato Mash.................................................................. 110

**Desserts and Snacks**.................................................................................................................................112
1. Triple Chocolate Coconut Cupcakes ......................................................................................... 113
2. Classic Italian Taralli ..................................................................................................................... 115
3. Anna's Blueberry Cake .................................................................................................................. 116
4. Orange Sunrise Bran Muffins with Creamy Dreamy Almond Milk .................................... 118
5. Cacao Goddess Pudding ............................................................................................................... 120
6. Fiori di Zucca .................................................................................................................................. 121
7. Lemon Poppy Seed Loaf ............................................................................................................... 122
8. Crazy-Crispy Kale Chips ................................................................................................................ 123
9. Banana Walnut Chocolate Chunk Cake .................................................................................... 124
10. Matcha Green Tea Pistachio Ice Cream ................................................................................... 125
11. Jennifer's Comforting Apple Crumble Cake ............................................................................ 126
12. Bliss Balance Brownie Balls ......................................................................................................... 128
13. Strawberry Shortcake Cupcakes................................................................................................. 129
14. AmoreTella Chocolate Spread .................................................................................................... 131
15. Cheese Scones ................................................................................................................................ 132
16. Chocolate Raspberry Valentine Cake ....................................................................................... 134
17. Zucchini Cranberry Loaf .............................................................................................................. 136

**About The Author**....................................................................................................................................138

# Acknowledgements

All that I am, I am because someone has loved me to it, through it, in spite of it or because of it. I am rich with treasures that transcend the material realm, because of you.

In particular, with all my heart, I would like to thank those who have believed in me and supported me with this bold vision of mine: a *vegan* new world.

My most sincere and abundant thanks to:

**Stéphane Bensoussan**, for planting this seed, and seeing this potential in me. You change lives.

**Mommy Lina**, for nudging me every day to complete this project and inspiring me since early childhood with your tantalizing dishes. Also, thank you for your boundless practical support, editing skills, expert cooking knowledge and devoted taste-testing! Most of all, thank you for the laughs! I could not have done this, any of it, without you.

**My treasure, my sister Felicia**, for loving me so fiercely and for always being so enthusiastic about my cooking, even when the culinary experiments clearly failed! Thank you so much for the rarest gift of all: unconditional love and support.

**Richard Harris**, for enduring my ups and downs, my ins and outs and my this and that, all these years. Thank you for being my best friend. Also, thank you so much for your invaluable help with editing this book. You've made it so much better.

**Ron Harris,** thank you for crossing my path and offering me your artistic eye and expertise in photography. You helped me make this book the best it could be with these gorgeous photos!

**Alexander von Ness**, at **Nessgraphica**, thank you so much for your incredible work on my book cover. I asked you for the most beautiful book cover in the world, and you gave me just that!

**Mike Reinharz, Chris Georgieff,** and everyone at **Into The Light Marketing** and **Vegan Carnivore**, for all your support and hard work at creating my exquisite logo.

**Marsh Engle**, for seeing a greatness in me when I did not see it myself, and for helping me find my voice.

**Joe Albanese,** for your loyal friendship, support, and never giving up on me no matter how many phone calls go missed!

**Alexandra Sidarous, Pierina Timeo, Freddy Cristinziano** and **Alberto Calzetta** for your precious friendships and support.

**Omar Yeret Hernandez Ponce,** gracias por seguir el alacrán y a las cucarachas, y entrar en mi vida.

**Rachel Levy Brown**, thank you for all your kindness and support. Thank you for seeing my heart and reminding me of my courage.

**Donna De Luca,** for seeing me.

**Olivia Deane**, **Tasha Deane**, **Katrina Deane-Riggio** and **Kara Deane** at **Sociale**, for believing in me, constantly encouraging me and strongly supporting my work. Thank you, also, for the opportunity to work with **Sociale**.

**Dino Martinez**, **Eddie Mah**, and **Rob Fleming**, thank you, my heroes, my champions, *real* men of this world for all that you do every day for the animals. Your friendship and support mean the world to me, and your presence in my life makes this journey less lonely.

**Isabelle Gagnon**, thank you, for inspiring me every day and for believing in me.

**Jennifer Horvath**, for being a strong supporter of my work and loving to eat all that I so love to cook.

**Santino Coco**, thank you, for provoking my awakening from emotional stupor.

**Papa, Antonio Amore**, grazie per essere aperto a questo nuovo modo di mangiare.

**Norma Barbaro**, for always treating me like I am someone special. Thank you for your kind and generous heart!

**Trisha Pope**, for being a wise tree of tremendous knowledge, serenity and compassion. Thank you for all that you have taught me in sound healing and in nurturing my clairvoyance. Thank you also for your guidance and inspiration.

**Dr. Josie Buttice**, for your passion and vision in natural holistic health. I learned so much from you and apply that knowledge every day!

**Antonio Di Florio**, thank you for all you taught me about garlic, much needed knife skills, especially with dicing tomatoes for bruschetta, and for the important clarification on the difference between a shallot and a green onion. Especially, thank you for being a catalyst in my spiritual development, helping me see the chains, and assisting me in breaking free.

**Kim Mecca**, for your regular check-ins, love, encouragement and unique insights. Thank you, especially, for inspiring me.

**Dr. Barbara Black**, for taking such excellent care of me all these years and always having my best interests in mind.

**Pina Ciccarelli**, for loving me so sincerely and always encouraging me!

**Antonio Di Petrillo** and **Debbie Mendonca**, for your friendships, your sensitivity, for supporting my work and for eagerly adopting this vegan way of life!

**Magda Viezel**, for your gentle, sincere smile, and for reminding me of my worth, in much darker times.

**Paula Engels**, for patiently helping me notice, and shift my focus.

**My beloved Gioia-Mia**, my angel who wears a dog disguise in this incarnation, thank you for teaching me that the only difference between you and a calf, you and a pig, you and a chicken, is the degree to which my heart is acquainted with these incarnations at this time.

**My brave Ganesha**, love embodied as a cat. Thank you for removing the nuisance of allergies so that we could live together as the One Love we were always meant to be. Thank you, especially, for giving me a second chance to love you better.

**My little girls, Bhakti and Vida**, your sweet kitty glances and cuddles break my heart open a little more each day.

**My two foster babies, Shalom and Aloha**, thank you for the innocence and purity you bring to my life, and for the tests of my patience and endurance!

**My budgie boys, Chant and Flash**, thank you for the live orchestra, my sound healing, every day.

Infinite gratitude to the great spiritual teachers who have transformed me, in particular: **His Divine Grace A.C. Bhaktivedanta Swami Prabhupada, Gurumayi Chidvilasananda, Maharishi Mahesh Yogi, Mother Teresa, Mahatma Gandhi** and **Albert Einstein**.

To my weekly column readers at Forget The Box, my followers on Twitter and Facebook, and my students who take my workshops and courses, thank you for hearing my voice, my pleas for compassion towards all beings, and for delighting with me over these vegan creations.

Lastly, endless gratitude to Divine Inspiration and guidance from God, and from all beings, physical and non-physical, human and non-human. My greatest bliss lies in our Oneness.

# Preface

*It is our duty to illumine the earth, as the stars do the night sky.*

I always loved cooking, but working as a corporate lawyer, as I did in the past, wasn't exactly conducive to putting together nutritious meals that took longer to prepare than making toast. I simply had no time to worry about nutrition and food preparation!

Due to a lifetime of stoic suppression of my basic bodily needs like rest, play and healthy eating, I got very sick. I struggled for a long time, trying to hide my devastating exhaustion from everyone, but it became almost impossible for me to get out of bed. I had the impression that I was crawling into my office, and my mental fog made it impossible for me to provide the excellence, precision and accuracy absolutely necessary for my work as a lawyer. With the medical doctors at a loss as to how to help me, I decided to take matters into my own hands and started learning about nutrition.

In pursuit of what was best for me to restore my health, I discovered the horrors of factory farming, the unbearable hell of treating animals like commodities. Quickly, actually overnight, I became a vegan, which means I cut out all animal products from my diet. Not only meat, I also eliminated fish, eggs, and all dairy. That was about five years ago. I continued researching and became positive I had made the healthiest choice not only for myself, but for the animals and the planet as a whole.

You see, it became clear to me that the paradigm had shifted. It is no longer only about what's good for me, it is about what's good for us, for you are me and I am you, and all there is, is us. We are One and what we do to them, we are doing to us.

My love for cooking exploded with this newfound truth. I felt so good ethically, spiritually and morally about my food choices and I was confident my body would start responding positively as well. It has been a long road back to health, but I have since accepted that life itself is the healing journey, and all our choices, including what we put into our bodies, can either facilitate this journey or deter us from it.

Now that I have made the connection, I don't eat animals for the same reason as I don't eat humans. To me, there is no difference between humans and animals, for we are all souls, in different physical disguises. I know that animals value their lives, their relationships, and their freedom to run and play as much as humans do. They feel a wide range of emotions just like we do. I want to create a better world for all animals and that, in turn, means a better world for everyone.

Thankfully, some of us are choosing to expand into this new paradigm of heart-centered living. However, many of us still suffer from a profound disconnect from one another and from God. The reason we are capable of the enslavement, torture and murder of other beings, humans and non-humans alike, is that we have lost touch with our Oneness. We perceive the "other" as separate from the "me"; however, this is inaccurate, a mere construct of the dualistic nature of the physical realm. There is no "me" versus "you". I am another you; you are another me.

This is the fundamental reason we participate in the suffering of other beings, and we must acknowledge it, see through the illusion of separateness, and reconnect once again to our hearts, to our divinity, to one another, to all of creation.

Make no mistake, anyone who purchases a slab of flesh, an egg, or a container of milk, has slit the throat of a being who begged for mercy, with terror in her eyes. Karmically, there is no difference between a butcher and his customer. To withhold mercy, I tell you, is the gravest action of cruelty there is and the karma wheel of suffering goes on. We now live in an age where much information is available to us. We can choose to look and act, or we can choose ignorance and pretend not to know, or delude ourselves that what is going on is OK because it has always been this way, or because the government will regulate it, or because my doctor tells me I need it, or because a huge yearly marketing campaign tells me it does a body good, etc. We were granted the ability to think and reason, why not think for ourselves? When we are presented with uncomfortable facts, when we witness suffering, it is an invitation from God to make a difference. We have several karmic invitations per day to display the state of our evolution in compassion. What do you choose to do?

It is time to take full responsibility for all our actions. It is time to become aware. It is time to choose compassion. It is time to make a difference, because we all have that luxury – to choose, whereas animals do not. We were born, each one of us, to shine with compassion. It is our duty to illumine the earth, as the stars do the night sky. Compassion for all beings is evolution.

*Cooking with Amore* is a personal odyssey back to wellness, a journey of self-discovery and my way of making this world a more peaceful place. My goal with this cookbook is to show you how easy and delicious vegan cooking can be. I believe the exploitation of animals is completely unnecessary and a result of the lack of knowledge of satisfying alternatives. With this cookbook, I present you an abundance of tasty, fully plant-based recipes!

I am called to teach you the bliss of vegan cooking. I am called to show you how scrumptious, nutritious and accessible it is to adopt a kind diet. I am called to provoke the compassion in you. Follow me. I found a blissful way to health, well-being and spiritual evolution!

Let's cook with amore.

Maria Amore
June 2013

*"I am not afraid. I was born to do this." ~Joan of Arc*

## Tips from Amore's Kitchen

1. *Water*

Water that is as pure as possible is always best for drinking and to use for any recipe. I have a reverse osmosis system in my home and in my opinion, it is worth the investment. The water not only tastes better, but it is free from many, hopefully most, impurities. Also, if you have access to fresh spring water, this is a great way to make use of nature's bounty.

2. *Salt*

Unrefined salt has many trace minerals that our bodies need, up to 80 or 90 depending on where it is harvested. My favorite is pink Himalayan salt, and that's what I use in all my recipes. In my opinion, Himalayan salt and any sea salt is a healthier choice than highly refined table salt. The quantities in these recipes are based on Himalayan salt and may vary depending on which salt you use. Some of my recipes suggest quantities, which you can adjust depending on your taste and health needs, and for other recipes, I leave it up to you to decide.

3. *Olive Oil*

We are looking for olive oil that is processed as little as possible. Whenever I call for olive oil in my recipes, I always mean extra-virgin, first cold pressed olive oil and organic, if possible. Olive oil should be used almost exclusively in raw recipes or for cooking at very low temperatures since it easily denatures with heat. For raw recipes, I also enjoy the health benefits of flaxseed oil. For stovetop cooking or for baking, I usually use grapeseed or coconut oil.

4. *Parsley and Basil*

For me, dried parsley and basil usually don't do the trick in recipes. Whereas with some other herbs a lot of the flavor remains when dried, with parsley and basil that isn't the case. Parsley and basil are so much more flavorful when they are fresh, especially when making tomato sauce for example. I do make use of dried basil on occasion in some recipes, but I never use dried parsley. Also, I believe that flat-leaf (Italian) parsley is tastier than the curly-leaf variety, so I always use flat-leaf parsley in my recipes. With respect to basil, I specify when to use dried or fresh basil in my recipes for best results.

5. *Spices*

Spices are truly the spice of life! Properly used, they have the power to transform the blandest of recipes into a culinary masterpiece. Experiment with as wide a variety of spices as possible. Keep in mind that your dishes will only be as good as the ingredients you use to make them. This includes the quality of the spices. Use the best quality spices you can find and afford, for best results. In my recipes, when I call for spices or herbs, I always mean dried and ground spices, unless I specify otherwise.

6. *Organic Versus Non-Organic*

Organic produce means it is grown without the use of harmful chemicals and is free from genetic modification. I believe that this is desirable for our health, and the health of the whole planet. Nature knows best and therein lies its healing power. Whenever possible, use organic ingredients. In my opinion, a few things should always be purchased organic, such as corn and soy products. You can also consult the *Clean Fifteen/Dirty Dozen List* online at: **www.ewg.org** for information on which fruits and vegetables are best purchased organic.

7. *Tofu*

Tofu is like a sponge, waiting for you to provide something tasty for it to absorb. I hear so many people claim they do not like tofu, but I am confident that they just haven't learned how to properly flavor it with a delicious marinade, for example. When you purchase firm tofu, remove it from the package, rinse it briefly and then place it on paper towels with a compress on top (a plate for example) to absorb all the excess liquid. This little trick will get the tofu ready to absorb the marinade more fully and add to the tastiness of the dish. Also, whenever I use tofu in my recipes, I always use organic.

8. *Agave Nectar and Other Natural Sweeteners*

There is a lot written about agave nectar and not all of it is positive! We do know that it has a lower glycemic index than many other sweeteners; however some versions of this natural plant sweetener are highly processed. When buying agave nectar, try to get as unprocessed a product as possible and look for the organic and raw version. **Stevia** and **Lakanto** are other plant-based, natural, low glycemic options for sweetening recipes.

9. *Bread Crumbs and Croutons*

As you will see in this cookbook, I make my own bread crumbs and croutons so that I can control exactly what goes in them. Commercial brands often have preservatives and refined salt. Also, we don't know what type of bread was used. To make bread crumbs, I allow my bread to dry and harden for several days and then grate it in the food processor or blender until it becomes powdery. After that, I add my own Himalayan salt and seasonings, depending on the recipe I am making. For croutons, as you will see, I bake cubes of bread with my desired seasoning.

10. *Broth*

For similar reasons as making my own bread crumbs, I also make my own broth. I have provided a simple, versatile recipe for a vegetable broth in this cookbook.

11. *Salad Dressing*

Again, why buy a commercial product with processed and undesirable ingredients when you can make a wholesome version with fresh and tasty ingredients in no time? Your health and taste buds will thank you for taking the extra few minutes to whip up your own dressing.

12. *Garlic*

Garlic is a gift from nature: an antibiotic, antiseptic and antiviral all in one! I use garlic generously (I'm Italian, after all!) for the flavor it adds to dishes and for all of its health benefits. When using garlic, it is important to slice it in half and remove the germ. The germ is what causes some people to experience heartburn and also contributes to that distinctive breath aroma! To a lesser degree, but also advisable, the germ from onions may also be removed.

13. *Soaking and Cooking Beans*

I don't use beans or chickpeas from a can in any of my recipes. I prefer to buy dried beans and soak them for several hours before cooking them. I soak the beans and chickpeas overnight with a bay leaf and a piece of kombu (sea vegetable). I then cook them together with the bay leaf and kombu, removing them after about 30 minutes. This method eliminates the gas-forming effects of these foods. While the beans cook, skimming and discarding the foam will also help this process. Try these tricks and you'll notice a huge difference. Eat beans and rest assured, with Amore's tips! Keep in mind that, for convenience, you can cook a big batch of beans, drain and let them cool, and then freeze them for future recipes.

14. *Always Make a Recipe Your Own*

A recipe, in my opinion, is intended to be a guideline and hopefully a source of inspiration. Be creative and make it your own by adding or subtracting, or substituting ingredients which you prefer over others or which are more readily available to you. Most importantly, if you have allergies or an intolerance to certain ingredients in my recipes, please experiment with substitutes. It is always possible!

15. *Ovens*

My oven is not super powerful and by no means an industrial one. All the cooking times in this cookbook are based on my oven which may vary with yours. You can always be watchful and perform a "toothpick test" to see how your creation is coming along (insert the toothpick into the center and see if it comes out dry). If you have a powerful oven, you may need less cooking time than is indicated in the recipes here.

16. *Metric Conversions and Equivalents*

I have included metric conversions for your convenience throughout the book. These are approximate values. When I used cups or spoons to measure the amounts, I converted these into liters and milliliters.

17. *Strange Ingredients I've Never Heard of ...*

Especially if you are new to a vegan diet, there may be ingredients in my recipes that you have never heard of, like nutritional yeast or tempeh, for example. This is completely normal! I too had to learn many new things when I changed my diet. I shop for groceries at my local health food store and they have all the ingredients I use in these recipes. If one sounds unfamiliar, ask about it at your nearest health food store, or write me a note at **withamore@gmail.com** and I will be more than pleased to assist you. Furthermore, depending on where you live in the world, you may not have access to certain ingredients all the time. Be creative and substitute as best you can. You may also take a chance and omit an ingredient if it is impossible for you to get it.

18. *Cooking with Amore*

To me, cooking with love is necessarily vegan because it removes as much of the violence as possible from the act of preparing food and eating. In addition, I believe that cooking with love requires a sense of presence. We need to be fully engaged, with all our senses, when we are cooking, and essentially become one with the dish we are preparing. Not only do we absorb the energy of our food, but we transmit energy to it as well; be mindful of the emotions and thoughts you bring into the kitchen, as they will be directly transferred to the food. Most importantly, always remember this: Love is essentially the only irreplaceable ingredient in any dish. Everything else can be substituted.

*"If I sing when I cook, the food will be happy." ~Pasquale Carpino*

# Soups

# Mega Protein Bowl: Kale and Bean Stew

*This hearty and delicious stew will keep you warm and satiated on those cold winter days. Stock up on vitamins, minerals and plant-based protein just from one heaping bowl of stew.*

**Ingredients:**
*Makes approximately 6 servings*

2 tablespoons (30 ml) grapeseed oil
2 cloves of garlic, minced
1 onion, chopped
1 tablespoon (15 ml) fresh ginger, minced
1 sweet potato, chopped
1 carrot, chopped
1 celery stalk, chopped
2 turnips, chopped
1 large bunch of green or red curly kale, stems removed, chopped
2 cups (500 ml) red kidney beans or black beans presoaked and cooked (see "Soaking and Cooking Beans" section on page 17)
½ cup (125 ml) frozen organic corn, cooked
2 cups (500 ml) of vegetable broth (see recipe on page 30) and 1 cup (250 ml) water (or 3 cups (750 ml) water only)
1 teaspoon (5 ml) cumin
1 teaspoon (5 ml) cardamom
1 teaspoon (5 ml) turmeric
1 cup (250 ml) fresh parsley, chopped
Himalayan salt and black pepper to taste

**Method:**
1. In a large pot, heat oil. Add garlic, onions and ginger, with a pinch of salt, and sauté for 3 to 4 minutes. Add sweet potato, carrot, celery, turnips, another pinch of salt and sauté for 5 minutes. Add kale, beans and corn and sauté another 5 minutes. Add broth and water (or just water), salt, pepper, cumin, cardamom, and turmeric. Reduce heat to simmer.
2. After 20 minutes, scoop up 1 ½ cups (375 ml) of stew and place it in a small bowl to cool slightly. Once cooled, pour it into your blender. Blend until creamy.
3. Pour mixture back into pot. Continue to simmer for 20 minutes or until all vegetables are soft. Turn off heat. Stir in chopped parsley. Taste test to see if additional salt is required. Add black pepper if desired.
4. Scoop into bowl and serve warm.

*"The intention of every other piece of prose may be discussed and even mistrusted, but the purpose of a cookery book is one and unmistakable. Its object can conceivably be no other than to increase the happiness of mankind." ~Joseph Conrad*

## Autumn Harvest Bowl: Three Squash Soup

*I love the comforting warmth, delicate sweetness and grounding feeling I get from indulging myself with this delicious soup. Everything feels just fine whenever I have a bowl of Three Squash Soup ...*

**Ingredients:**
*Makes approximately 4 servings*

1 small butternut squash
2 other varieties of small squash
3 tablespoons (45 ml) grapeseed oil or coconut oil
5 or 6 small potatoes, peeled, washed and chopped
3 cloves of garlic, minced
2 tablespoons (30 ml) of fresh parsley or cilantro, chopped
Himalayan salt and black pepper to taste

**Method:**
1. Preheat oven to 375°F (190°C).
2. Place the varieties of squash whole in a large glass casserole dish or on a strong baking sheet. Bake for 15 minutes to soften.
3. Remove from oven and cut the squash in half. Add 2 tablespoons (30 ml) of grapeseed oil to baking sheet and place squash face down. Bake for 25 minutes or until flesh is very soft. Remove from the oven and let cool.
4. Place potatoes, 1 clove minced garlic and salt, about ½ teaspoon (2.5 ml), in a pot with water and bring to a boil. Lower heat and cook for approximately 20 minutes or until potatoes are soft. Drain.
5. In a small pot, heat 1 tablespoon (15 ml) of grapesed oil. Add 2 cloves of minced garlic and sauté until golden. Set aside to cool.
6. Scoop out flesh from the squash into your food processor or blender. Add potatoes and browned garlic (including oil).
7. Add 1 cup (250 ml) of water, parsley and salt. Blend until creamy. If the mixture is too thick for your liking, add more water.
8. Transfer mixture to a large pot and heat on low. Taste test to check if more salt is desired. Garnish with black pepper and fresh parsley or cilantro. Serve warm.

## Bonnya's Potato and Garlic Soup

*Bonnya wrote to me all the way from India. She was looking for a satisfying soup recipe with ingredients that were accessible in her country. I created this in her honor! Here was her response when she made it for the first time:*

*"Dear Maria, this morning the first thing I did is I prepared the soup. It was mind-blowing! It kick-started our day with bundles of delight. It is a food for happiness. Hats off to you for your amazing creation. Thank you very much." ~Bonnya*

**Ingredients:**
*Makes approximately 6 servings*

10 small white potatoes, peeled, washed and chopped
1 large white onion, chopped
5 cloves of garlic, chopped
1 tablespoon (15 ml) of grapeseed oil
2 cups (500 ml) water (and more water to boil potatoes)
2 tablespoons (30 ml) dried chives
2 tablespoons (30 ml) nutritional yeast
Himalayan salt and black pepper to taste
Chopped fresh parsley to garnish

**Method:**
1. Place potatoes, onion, 1 tablespoon (15 ml) of salt and 1 clove of garlic in a large pot. Add enough water to cover the potatoes. Bring to a boil and lower heat. Cook until potatoes are soft, about 20 minutes. Drain water and let cool.
2. In a small pot, heat grapeseed oil and add remaining garlic. Sauté garlic until slightly golden. Remove from heat and let cool.
3. Once cooled, add boiled potatoes (with onion and garlic) and sautéed garlic (with oil) to a blender. Add 2 cups (500 ml) of water, chives and nutritional yeast. Blend well, until smooth and creamy. If mixture is too thick, add more water.
4. Before serving, transfer mixture to a pot and warm on stovetop. Taste test to see if more salt is desired.
5. Garnish with freshly ground black pepper and parsley if desired. Serve warm.

**"Tradition becomes our security, and when the mind is secure it is in decay." ~Jiddu Krishnamurti**

# Rapini Lentil Stew

*Lentils, when made in this fashion with mushrooms, fennel seed and steak spice, are so hearty and "meaty" that they can satisfy even the most discriminating non-vegans. Full of taste and nutrition, this lentil dish can be a complete meal on its own, or poured over noodles, steamed vegetables or rice is also delicious.*

### Ingredients:
*Makes approximately 6 servings*

3 tablespoons (45 ml) grapeseed oil
4 cloves garlic, minced
2 cups (500 ml) French lentils
2 cups (500 ml) homemade vegetable broth (see recipe on page 30) or 2 cups (500 ml) water
2 cups (500 ml) water (If using only water, 4 cups (1 L) in total)
1 bay leaf
2 cups (500 ml) mushrooms, chopped
1 tablespoon (15 ml) unsalted steak spice (for my homemade steak spice blend see page 69)
1 tablespoon (15 ml) oregano
1 teaspoon (5 ml) fennel seeds
4 cups (1 L) spinach or rapini, stems removed and chopped
1 teaspoon (5 ml) red chili flakes
½ cup (125 ml) fresh parsley or cilantro, chopped
Himalayan salt and black pepper to taste

### Method:
1. In a pot, heat 1 tablespoon (15 ml) of oil and 2 cloves of garlic over medium heat. Add lentils and stir, making sure they are coated with oil. After about 2 to 3 minutes, add broth and water (or just water). Add salt and bay leaf.
2. Once mixture boils, lower heat and let simmer for approximately 1 hour, partially covered. Taste test to make sure the lentils are soft.
3. While lentils are cooking, heat 1 tablespoon (15 ml) of oil and 1 clove of garlic in a saucepan. Add chopped mushrooms, steak spice, oregano, fennel seeds and salt. Cook over medium heat until mushrooms are soft, about 5 minutes. Set aside.
4. In another saucepan, heat 1 tablespoon (15 ml) of oil and 1 clove of garlic. Add chopped spinach or rapini. Add chili flakes and salt. Cook over medium heat until leaves are wilted and tender, about 5 minutes for spinach, 10 minutes for rapini. Set aside.
5. Once lentils are soft, remove bay leaf and discard. Add mushrooms and spinach or rapini to the pot. Garnish with chopped fresh parsley or cilantro. Can be served alone, or over rice, steamed vegetables or noodles. Serve warm.

# The Market Soup: Quinoa-Cream of Leek

*I love going to farmers' markets and picking up fresh leeks! This soup was inspired by one of those trips to the market. I came home with a bunch of beautiful leeks and set out to create a vegan cream of leek experience. I use quinoa to create the cream!*

**Ingredients:**
*Makes approximately 6 servings*

2 tablespoons (30 ml) grapeseed oil or coconut oil
3 cups (750 ml) of leek, chopped
1 onion, chopped
3 cloves of garlic, minced
1 large potato, chopped
½ cup (125 ml) of quinoa
3 cups (750 ml) water
3 cups (750 ml) vegetable broth (see recipe on page 30) or just 6 cups (1 ½ L) of water in total
⅓ cup (80 ml) fresh parsley or cilantro, chopped, and more for garnish if desired.
Himalayan salt and black pepper to taste

**Method:**
1. In a large pot, heat grapeseed oil over medium to low heat. Add leek, onion, garlic and potato. Sprinkle about a teaspoon of salt over vegetables. Cook for about 10 minutes covered, stirring frequently.
2. Add quinoa to vegetables and stir. Allow to cook together for about 5 minutes.
3. Add vegetable broth and water (or just 6 cups (1 ½ L) of water in total). Cover and bring to a boil.
4. Lower heat and simmer for 45 minutes to 1 hour, partially covered. Stir occasionally.
5. Turn heat off and add chopped parsley or cilantro
6. Let cool. Once cooled, blend in a blender. Taste test and add more salt if desired.
7. Transfer to pot and heat to serve. Garnish with more chopped fresh parsley or cilantro and a dash of black pepper, if desired. Serve warm.

*"Nothing will benefit human health and increase chances for survival of life on Earth as much as the evolution to a vegetarian diet." ~Albert Einstein*

## The Bucerias: Avocado Soup

*Everyone has the same reaction to this soup: "What?! Warm avocado?!" Oh yes, warm avocado and roasted garlic soup is heavenly, just like the small town of Bucerias, in Puerto Vallarta, Mexico, where this soup was inspired. I love you, Bucerias.*

### Ingredients:
*Makes approximately 3 servings*

1 tablespoon (15 ml) grapeseed oil
1 clove of garlic, minced
3 ripe avocados
3 tablespoons (45 ml) fresh cilantro, chopped

½ cup (125 ml) raw walnuts
½ cup (125 ml) water
½ teaspoon (2.5 ml) Himalayan salt

### Method:
1. In a small pot, heat grapeseed oil. Sauté garlic until slightly golden. Do not overcook. Allow to cool.
2. In a small bowl, mash avocados with a fork or masher. Add avocados, cilantro, walnuts, water, salt and browned garlic (with oil) to a food processor or blender. Blend until smooth and creamy. If mixture is too thick for your liking, add more water.
3. Transfer mixture to a pot and warm on low heat for a few minutes, stirring occasionally. Taste test to see if more salt is required.
4. Garnish with freshly ground black pepper, chopped walnuts and more chopped cilantro or parsley if desired. Serve warm.

# The India: Quinoa-Cream of Carrot

*For my cream of carrot soup, I create the cream with quinoa. If you don't have some homemade vegetable broth on hand, you can use water instead and this soup will still be wonderfully tasty. My choice of spices for this creation reminds me of the flavors and scents of Indian cuisine, which I adore. Let your taste buds be dazzled by mystical places abroad!*

### Ingredients:
Makes 6 to 8 servings

3 tablespoons (45 ml) grapeseed oil or coconut oil
4 cups (1 L) carrots, peeled and chopped
4 cloves of garlic, minced
1 tablespoon (15 ml) fresh ginger, chopped
½ teaspoon (2.5 ml) fennel seeds
½ teaspoon (2.5 ml) chili flakes (optional)
½ cup (125 ml) quinoa
2 cups (500 ml) vegetable broth (see recipe on page 30) or water

2 cups (500 ml) water (if using only water, 4 cups (1 L) in total)
1 teaspoon (5 ml) curry powder
½ teaspoon (2.5 ml) cumin
1 teaspoon (5 ml) turmeric
¼ teaspoon (1.25 ml) cayenne pepper (optional)
Fresh parsley and hot chili peppers, finely chopped for garnish if desired
Himalayan salt and black pepper to taste

### Method:
1. In a large pot, heat oil over medium heat. Add carrots, garlic, ginger, one teaspoon (5 ml) salt, fennel seeds and chili flakes and sauté for about 10 to 15 minutes covered, stirring frequently.
2. Add quinoa to vegetables and cook together for 5 minutes. Add vegetable broth, water and all remaining spices. Cover and bring to a boil.
3. Lower heat and simmer for 1 to 1 ½ hours. Stir occasionally.
4. Turn off heat and add a handful of chopped fresh parsley to the soup. Let cool. Once cooled, blend in a blender. Add more water if too thick for your liking.
5. Transfer to pot and heat on low heat. Add salt and black pepper to taste. Garnish with chopped fresh parsley and hot chili peppers, if desired. Serve warm.

*"The freedom of all is essential to my freedom."* ~Mikhail Bakunin

## A Vegan's Italian Minestrone

*Minestrone is a classic, thick and hearty Italian stew. It is made with any vegetables which are in season, or even leftovers from other meals! It is common to add beans and pasta or rice to minestrone, and quite often some type of meat is added as well. Not a problem for us vegans! There are many vegan "meats" on the market. In this minestrone I used a spicy Italian vegan sausage and it was scrumptious!*

**Ingredients:**
*Makes 5 to 6 servings*

4 tablespoons (60 ml) grapeseed oil
1 package vegan sausage of your choice (about 4 large sausages)
2 potatoes, washed but not peeled and chopped
2 onions, chopped
6 cloves of garlic, minced
1 cup (250 ml) mushrooms, chopped or halved
1 teaspoon (5 ml) oregano
1 teaspoon (5 ml) fennel seeds
2 carrots, peeled and chopped
1 celery, chopped
1 tomato, chopped
1 cup (250 ml) organic corn, frozen

1 cup (250 ml) peas, frozen
½ cup (125 ml) kidney beans, cooked (see section on "Soaking and Cooking Beans" on page 17)
¾ cup (180 ml) strained tomatoes
4 cups (1 L) Swiss chard or spinach stems removed and chopped
3 cups (750 ml) water
1 cup (250 ml) fresh parsley, chopped
1 cup (250 ml) cooked pasta noodles of your choice (I use brown rice noodles for a gluten-free dish.)
Himalayan salt and black pepper to taste

**Method:**
1. Preheat oven to 450°F (230°C).
2. Add 2 tablespoons (30 ml) of grapeseed oil to a large casserole dish. Add chopped sausages, potatoes, 1 onion, 2 cloves of garlic and mushrooms. Sprinkle oregano, fennel seeds and about 1 teaspoon (5 ml) of salt over top. Cover dish with aluminum foil, perforated in a few spots to let steam out as it bakes.
3. Bake for 25 minutes. Turn sausages and vegetables after 15 minutes. Once cooked, remove from oven and set aside.
4. On the stovetop, heat 2 tablespoons (30 ml) of grapeseed oil on medium heat in a large pot. Add 1 onion, 4 cloves of garlic, chopped carrots, celery and tomato. Sauté for 7 or 8 minutes while stirring. Add corn, peas, beans and strained tomatoes. Continue sautéing for 3 to 4 minutes. Add Swiss chard or spinach, sprinkle about a teaspoon of salt and stir until wilted.
5. Add water and bring to a boil. Lower heat to simmer.
6. Simmer for 30 minutes, partially covered, stirring occasionally. Turn off heat.
7. Add parsley to minestrone and stir.
8. Prepare pasta noodles. Drain and set aside.
9. Add cooked sausage and vegetables to minestrone pot. Add noodles. Stir.
10. Add more salt if desired and black pepper. Serve warm.

## Split Pea Soup with Smoked Kale

*I created a vegan split pea soup so delicious that it is addictive! I added a little kale and liquid smoke to this soup, optional ingredients, which I chose in order to mimic the familiar and much loved smoky flavor of the non-vegan variety.*

### Ingredients:
*Makes approximately 6 to 8 servings*

2 tablespoons (30 ml) of grapeseed oil
2 onions, chopped
4 cloves of garlic, minced
2 carrots, chopped
2 celery stalks, chopped
2 cups of kale, stems removed and chopped
2 teaspoons (10 ml) Himalayan salt (or more to taste)
½ teaspoon (2.5 ml) chili flakes
4 cups (1 L) dry yellow split peas

8 to 10 cups (2 to 2 ½ L) of water
1 bay leaf
1 teaspoon (5 ml) cumin
1 teaspoon (5 ml) turmeric
1 teaspoon (5 ml) oregano
¼ teaspoon (1.25 ml) cayenne pepper
1 tablespoon (15 ml) liquid smoke (optional)
Black pepper to taste

### Method:
1. Heat oil on medium heat. Add onion, garlic and a pinch of salt. Sauté for 5 minutes while stirring.
2. Stir in carrots, celery, kale, 1 teaspoon (5 ml) of salt and chili flakes. Sauté another 5 minutes.
3. Add split peas. Sauté for 2 minutes.
4. Add water, 2 teaspoons (10 ml) salt, and bay leaf. Bring to a boil. Lower heat and simmer for about 50 to 60 minutes. Split peas are cooked when they are very soft and purée-like.
5. Add all remaining spices and liquid smoke (optional).
6. Turn heat off and discard bay leaf. Add more salt if desired. Serve warm.

*"What emerges from the silence is the deafening sound of an old world disintegrating."*
~Marianne Williamson

# Quinoa-Cream of Broccoli

*One last soup using my quinoa method to create the creaminess. I know cream of broccoli is a very common favorite for cream soup lovers so I had to include this one! Enjoy the smooth texture and soothing warmth with this easy soup recipe!*

**Ingredients:**
*Makes approximately 5 to 6 servings*

2 tablespoons (30 ml) grapeseed oil
4 cloves of garlic, minced
2 onions, chopped
5 cups (1 ¼ L) of broccoli, chopped into small pieces
½ cup (125 ml) quinoa
6 cups (1 ½ L) of water
1 cup (250 ml) fresh parsley, chopped
Himalayan salt
Black pepper and chopped fresh parsley for garnish, if desired

**Method:**
1. In a large pot, heat grapeseed oil over medium heat. Add garlic and onions. Sauté for about 3 or 4 minutes. Add broccoli. Sprinkle about a teaspoon (5 ml) of salt over vegetables. Cook for 10 minutes, covered, stirring frequently.
2. Add quinoa to vegetables and stir. Allow to cook together for about 5 minutes.
3. Add water, cover and bring to a boil.
4. Lower heat and simmer for 45 minutes to 1 hour, partially covered. Stir occasionally.
5. Turn heat off and add chopped parsley.
6. Let cool. Once cooled, blend in a blender. Taste test and add more salt if desired. Transfer to pot and heat on low to serve. Garnish with more chopped fresh parsley and a dash of black pepper, if desired. Serve warm.

## Lina's Vegetable Broth

*Inspired by a dream in which my mom told me she missed having broth now that we were vegan, I created this versatile vegetable broth and named it after her. It is delicious as a base for a soup (just add your favorite noodles and spinach or other vegetables like peas and corn), or to flavor other dishes, such as rice or quinoa. A tasty broth can indeed be achieved solely with vegetables! When you are using vegetables for your other recipes, keep the stalks to make this broth. You may also freeze the vegetable stalks to make the broth at a later date.*

### Ingredients:

*Makes approximately 6 to 7 cups of broth*

- At least 4 cups (1 L) of green vegetable stalks of your choice, chopped
- 2 or 3 carrots, peeled and chopped in half
- 1 or 2 celery stalks
- 3 or 4 cloves of garlic, halved
- 1 or 2 onions, quartered
- 8 to 10 cups (2 to 2 ½ L) water
- 1 to 2 tablespoons (15 to 30 ml) Himalayan salt
- 1 tablespoon (15 ml) oregano

### Method:

1. Boil all the ingredients together for at least 1 hour.
2. Cool. Strain and discard vegetables, except carrots and onion.
3. Mash carrots and onion and add back to the broth if making a soup base (optional). You may also add chopped spinach at this time.
4. If making soup, bring to a boil and add noodles of your choice.
5. If you don't use the broth right away, you can store it in Mason jars for your other recipes.

*"The miracle of your mind isn't that you can see the world as it is. It's that you can see the world as it isn't." ~Kathryn Schulz*

# Salads, Dips and Pâtés

## The Mayan: Tomato Cacao Salad

*So prized, cacao was known as mayan gold. Here I took a classic Italian tomato salad and transformed it with cacao nibs!*

**Ingredients:**
*Makes approximately 4 servings*

8 large ripe tomatoes (preferably from your own garden!), chopped
½ white onion, thinly sliced (optional)
½ cup (125 ml) fresh baby basil (also called Dwarf Greek Basil, a small leaf variety of basil)
3 tablespoons (45 ml) olive oil
1 tablespoon (15 ml) dried oregano
¼ cup (60 ml) raw cacao nibs
1 teaspoon (5 ml) Himalayan salt

**Method:**
1. Combine all ingredients in a large bowl. Toss gently. Serve at room temperature with your favorite bread.

*"Learn the rules like a pro, so you can break them like an artist."* ~Pablo Picasso

## Bean and Celery Salad

*There's a trick I know for making beans and chickpeas friendlier for our digestive track. See my paragraph "Soaking and Cooking Beans" in the section "Tips From Amore's Kitchen" for some useful tricks. This is my favorite recipe for a simple kidney bean salad with the accompanying fresh crispiness of celery.*

**Ingredients:**
*Makes approximately 6 servings*

2 cups dried kidney beans
1 bay leaf
1 strip of kombu
1 cup (250 ml) celery, chopped
¼ cup (60 ml) fresh parsley or cilantro, chopped
4 green onions, chopped
2 tablespoons (30 ml) olive or flaxseed oil

½ teaspoon (2.5 ml) red chili flakes
1 teaspoon (5 ml) oregano
2 tablespoons (30 ml) balsamic vinegar or juice from one lemon
1 tablespoon (15 ml) shelled hemp seeds
Himalayan salt and black pepper to taste

**Method:**
1. Soak beans overnight and cook them according to instructions in the section "Soaking and Cooking Beans" on page 17. Boil beans for a total of 1 to 1 ½ hours, or until beans are soft. Remove the bay leaf and kombu after about 20 minutes and discard. Skim the foam while cooking.
2. Once beans are soft, remove from heat and drain. Let cool.
3. Mix cooled beans and all other ingredients in large bowl, except hemp seeds.
4. Sprinkle hemp seeds for garnish. Serve at room temperature or chilled.

# Cheeky Chickpea Salad

*Chickpeas, also called garbanzo beans, are so delicious, nutritious and versatile! Here is a quick and easy salad recipe which you can serve alone, as a side dish or over your favorite greens, such as fresh arugula lettuce. Follow the same soaking and cooking tips that I mentioned previously with the bean salad recipe.*

**Ingredients:**
*Makes approximately 6 servings*

2 cups dried chickpeas
1 bay leaf
1 piece of kombu
1 celery stalk, chopped
6 cherry tomatoes, quartered
3 green onions, chopped
1 garlic clove, minced
2 tablespoons (30 ml) olive oil
2 tablespoons (30 ml) balsamic vinegar or juice from one lemon
1 tablespoon (15 ml) oregano
⅓ cup (80 ml) fresh parsley, chopped
Himalayan salt and freshly ground black pepper to taste

**Method:**
1. Soak chickpeas overnight and cook them according to instructions in the section "Soaking and Cooking Beans" on page 17. Boil chickpeas for a total of 1 to 1 ½ hours, or until they are soft. Remove the bay leaf and kombu after about 20 minutes and discard. Skim the foam while cooking.
2. Remove from heat and drain all liquid. Allow to cool.
3. Mix cooled chickpeas and all other ingredients in large bowl.
4. Refrigerate for ½ hour for flavors to marinate. Serve chilled.

*"Everything is energy and that's all there is to it. Match the frequency of the reality you want and you cannot help but get that reality. It can be no other way. This is not philosophy. This is physics." ~Albert Einstein*

## Almond Arugula Pesto

*Certainly one of my favorite inventions and one which so many people have already gone nuts over! This pesto is so creamy and delicious you will not believe it's actually healthy! Incredibly versatile: try it with your favorite pasta, quinoa, as a dip for veggies, as a spread in sandwiches or even as a sauce in your spring rolls.*

**Ingredients:**
*Makes approximately 6 servings*

2 cups (500 ml) arugula
1 cup (250 ml) fresh parsley, chopped
1 garlic clove, minced
½ cup (125 ml) raw walnuts
¼ cup (60 ml) lemon juice
⅓ cup (80 ml) water
½ cup (125 ml) raw almonds, soaked for 1 hour

1 teaspoon (5 ml) oregano
1 ½ teaspoons (7.5 ml) Himalayan salt
½ teaspoon (2.5 ml) black pepper
¼ cup (60 ml) hemp seeds
¼ cup (60 ml) nutritional yeast
½ cup (125 ml) olive oil

**Method:**
1. Combine all ingredients in a food processor and blend until smooth and creamy.
2. Serve at room temperature. Alternatively, it can be warmed slightly or served chilled, depending on what you are serving it with.

# Classic Italian Potato Salad

*Italians typically do not use mayonnaise in their potato salad. Instead, they use their beloved extra-virgin olive oil, garlic and white vinegar. This is a classic summertime picnic favorite!*

**Ingredients:**
*Makes approximately 6 servings*

8 white or red potatoes
1 red bell pepper, chopped into small chunks
1 cup (250 ml) Moroccan black olives
2 cloves of garlic, minced
1 tablespoon (15 ml) oregano
4 tablespoons (60 ml) olive oil
5 tablespoons (75 ml) white vinegar
Red chili flakes, Himalayan salt and black pepper to taste

**Method:**
1. Wash potatoes thoroughly. Place them whole, unpeeled, in a large pot and add enough water to cover the potatoes. Bring to a boil.
2. Lower heat to medium and cook potatoes for about 25 minutes or until potatoes start to appear soft. You can test the texture of a potato with a fork or toothpick.
3. Drain hot water and fill pot with cold water to help potatoes cool.
4. Once cool, peel off the skin of each potato carefully with your fingers.
5. Rinse the potatoes with cool water. Slice each potato in half horizontally. Slice each half into another half. Cut the pieces of potato into small chunks and place into large bowl.
6. Add red pepper and all other ingredients. Stir gently. Allow flavors to marinate for at least 20 minutes. Serve at room temperature or slightly chilled.

*"To close your eyes will not ease another's pain."* ~Ancient Chinese Proverb

## The Sensualist: Roasted Eggplant and Pepper Delicacy

*Roasted eggplant and red bell pepper – so delicious it becomes a sensual experience. This dish is typically served with fresh bread as an appetizer, or in a sandwich.*

### Ingredients:
*Makes approximately 6 servings*

4 tablespoons (60 ml) grapeseed oil
3 eggplants, sliced in half
2 red bell peppers, tops sliced off
1 or 2 cloves of garlic, minced

2 tablespoons (30 ml) olive oil
Juice from one lemon
½ cup (125 ml) fresh parsley, chopped
Himalayan salt and freshly ground black pepper, to taste

### Method:
1. Preheat oven at 400°F (200°C).
2. Coat a large glass or porcelain baking dish with grapeseed oil.
3. Place eggplants and peppers cut-side down onto the oiled baking dish.
4. Bake uncovered for about 30 to 45 minutes, or until the flesh is very soft.
5. Remove from the oven and cover with aluminum foil. Allow to cool slowly, for at least one hour.
6. Once cooled, remove skins from the eggplants and peppers. Discard.
7. Shred the eggplants and peppers into thin strips and place in a colander to allow excess liquid to drain.
8. Transfer eggplants and peppers to a large bowl and mix in all other ingredients. Chill for ½ hour to allow flavors to marinate. Serve cold with your favorite bread, crackers, in a sandwich, or as is!

## A Vegan's Caesar Salad

*Vegans do not have to give up anything! In fact, being vegan is all about gaining: health, happiness and a feeling that you are helping the whole planet! Enjoy this completely vegan, completely delicious Caesar Salad! A tasty alternative is to use this dressing on kale or spinach.*

**Ingredients:**
*Makes approximately 2 to 4 servings*

1 head of Romaine lettuce, chopped
½ cup (125 ml) vegan mayonnaise
1 clove of garlic, crushed
3 tablespoons (45 ml) lemon juice
1 tablespoon (15 ml) Dijon mustard
¼ cup (60 ml) nutritional yeast

1 tablespoon (15 ml) wheat-free tamari
½ teaspoon (2.5 ml) coarse black pepper
½ cup (125 ml) croutons (see recipe below)
Garnish by sprinkling vegan bacon bits and vegan parmesan (see recipe below)

**Method:**
1. Place chopped Romaine lettuce in a large bowl. Set aside.
2. In a small bowl, whisk mayonnaise, crushed garlic, lemon juice, mustard, nutritional yeast, tamari and black pepper.
3. Pour dressing over lettuce and toss. Add croutons. Sprinkle bacon bits and parmesan over the salad.

*Vegan Parmesan*

**Ingredients:**
¼ cup (60 ml) raw cashews
¼ cup (60 ml) nutritional yeast

**Method:**
1. In a food processor, combine cashews and nutritional yeast. Blend until powdery.
2. Sprinkle over salad or any dish you like.

*Homemade Croutons*

**Ingredients:**
2 slices of bread, cubed
2 tablespoons (30 ml) balsamic vinegar
2 tablespoons (30 ml) olive oil
1 clove of garlic, minced (or powdered garlic)
1 tablespoon (15 ml) oregano
1 teaspoon (5 ml) Himalayan salt

**Method:**
1. Preheat oven to 350°F (180°C).
2. Slice bread into small cubes. Place bread cubes in a large casserole dish or baking sheet.
3. Drizzle balsamic vinegar and olive oil over bread. Sprinkle garlic, oregano, and salt.
4. Bake for 15 to 20 minutes or until bread is hard and crispy. Add to your salad or any dish you like.

*"We cannot do great things on this Earth, only small things with great love." ~Mother Teresa*

## Amore Veggie and Seed Pâté

*Dissatisfied with certain ingredients in the veggie pâtés on the market, I set out to create my own! So glad I did! This makes a big batch that you can store in the fridge and have ready for quick lunches all week long.*

### Ingredients:
*Makes approximately 8 servings*

1 cup (250 ml) onion, chopped
½ cup (125 ml) celery, chopped
1 cup (250 ml) red cabbage, chopped
1 cup (250 ml) carrots, chopped
2 cloves of garlic, finely minced
2 cups (500 ml) raw sunflower seeds, soaked for 1 to 2 hours
2 cups (500 ml) chickpeas, cooked and cooled (see tips in "Soaking and Cooking Beans" on page 17)
½ cup (125 ml) raw pumpkin seeds
⅓ cup (80 ml) ground flaxseed
⅓ cup (80 ml) shelled hemp seeds
¼ cup (60 ml) chia seeds
½ cup (125 ml) fresh parsley, finely chopped
Juice from 2 lemons

⅓ cup (80 ml) extra virgin olive oil
¾ cup (180 ml) water
1 teaspoon (5 ml) oregano
½ teaspoon (2.5 ml) dried basil
½ teaspoon (2.5 ml) cumin
2 to 3 teaspoons (10 to 15 ml) Himalayan salt
1 teaspoon (5 ml) mustard powder
1 teaspoon (5 ml) turmeric
½ teaspoon (2.5 ml) chili flakes
½ teaspoon (2.5 ml) black pepper
½ teaspoon (2.5 ml) paprika

### Method:
1. Combine all ingredients in a large bowl and mix well.
2. Process in small batches in a food processor, on high speed until ingredients are completely blended. Combine all processed batches in a large bowl and taste test to see if more salt or spices are desired.
3. Serve on your favorite bread, crackers, veggie slices or as a dip for raw veggies. Store in glass container for up to 5 days in refrigerator.

## String Bean Moroccan Olive Feast

*A salad so tasty it feels like a feast all on its own! This is a common summer favorite, often enjoyed when the garden is overflowing with luscious string beans, tomatoes and onions. Serve with your favorite bread for dipping into this tasty dressing!*

### Ingredients:

*Makes approximately 2 servings*
Bunch of green string beans, tips removed, if desired
2 small tomatoes, chopped
½ cup (125 ml) black Moroccan olives
½ onion, thinly sliced (optional)
½ garlic clove, minced
½ cup (125 ml) fresh parsley, chopped
1 teaspoon (5 ml) oregano
½ teaspoon (2.5 ml) red chili flakes
2 tablespoons (30 ml) olive oil
2 tablespoons (30 ml) balsamic vinegar
Himalayan salt and freshly ground black pepper to taste

### Method:
1. Steam or boil string beans. Do not overcook, as they are tastiest and most nutritious if cooked only slightly. Allow to cool.
2. Toss all ingredients gently in a large bowl.
3. Refrigerate for ½ hour to allow the flavors to marinate. Serve chilled.

*"It is no measure of health to be well adjusted to a profoundly sick society." ~Jiddu Krishnamurti*

# Maria's Heavenly Hummus

*Dissatisfied with some of the ingredients and with the bland taste of hummus on the market, I decided to create my own. I find the secret to a tasty hummus is in the choice of spices. Go wild and experiment with different spices and see how your palate reacts! Adding a roasted red bell pepper to this hummus recipe is a tasty alternative.*

**Ingredients:**
*Makes approximately 6 servings*

2 cups (500 ml) dried chickpeas
1 bay leaf
1 piece of kombu
1 garlic clove, finely minced
Juice from one lemon
3 tablespoons (45 ml) olive oil
3 tablespoons (45 ml) tahini
1 ½ teaspoons (7.5 ml) Himalayan salt (or more to taste)
¼ cup (60 ml) water
½ teaspoon (2.5 ml) freshly ground black pepper
1 teaspoon (5 ml) cumin
1 teaspoon (5 ml) paprika
1 teaspoon (5 ml) turmeric
3 tablespoons (45 ml) fresh parsley, chopped

**Method:**
1. Soak chickpeas overnight and cook them according to instructions in the section "Soaking and Cooking Beans" on page 17. Boil chickpeas for a total of 1 to 1 ½ hours, or until they are soft. Remove the bay leaf and kombu after about 20 minutes and discard. Skim the foam while cooking.
2. Drain and let cool.
3. Combine all ingredients in a blender or food processor. If mixture is too thick to blend, add more water until mixture blends easily on high speed. Blend until desired consistency is achieved.
4. Serve with crackers, bread, as a dip for veggies or as a sauce for your vegan burgers!

## Quinoa Chia Crunch Salad

*This is one of my favorite quinoa dishes! I love this one not only for the taste, but also for the crunch! Again and again, we can make a meal out of salad, and that meal can be a complete protein, along with other vital nutrients.*

**Ingredients:**
*Makes approximately 5 to 6 servings*

2 cups (500 ml) quinoa
3 cups (750 ml) water
1 ½ cups (375 ml) fresh parsley, chopped
1 small cucumber, chopped
½ cup (125 ml) green onion, chopped
1 garlic clove, minced
8 cherry tomatoes, quartered
1 small bell pepper, chopped (optional)
½ cup (125 ml) lemon juice
½ cup (125 ml) olive oil
1 tablespoon (15 ml) flaxseed oil or ground
¼ cup (60 ml) chia seeds
¼ cup (60 ml) raw sunflower seeds
¼ cup (60 ml) shelled hemp seeds
Himalayan salt and black pepper to taste

**Method:**
1. Add quinoa and water to a large pot and bring to a boil (1 ½ cups (375 ml) of water for every cup (250 ml) of quinoa). Simmer (covered) until all water is absorbed (about 10 to 15 minutes). Remove from heat and allow cooked quinoa time to cool – at least 2 hours.
2. Mix quinoa and all ingredients in a large bowl. Refrigerate for 1 hour before serving to allow the flavors to marinate.

*"Choose to inhale. Do not breathe simply to exist." ~Mattie Stepanek*

# Kim's Asian Flavors Cabbage Salad

*Look at this salad: a true feast for the eyes, as much as for the palate! My friend Kim loves this salad so much that I named it after her. Truth be told, everyone is really crazy about this dish! Lime, tamari, sesame oil and sesame seeds add that irresistible Asian flavor to a coleslaw-style salad.*

### Ingredients:
*Makes approximately 5 to 6 servings*

1 small head of green cabbage, shredded
4 small carrots, grated
1 small red onion, thinly sliced
½ red bell pepper, thinly sliced
½ green pepper, thinly sliced
2 small red chili peppers, finely chopped
1 avocado, chopped (optional)
1 tablespoon (15 ml) ginger, shredded
1 tablespoon (15 ml) raw sesame seeds
2 teaspoons (10 ml) black sesame seeds

### Dressing:
Juice from one lime
2 teaspoons (10 ml) sesame oil, raw or toasted, as desired
¼ cup (60 ml) rice wine vinegar
2 tablespoons (30 ml) wheat-free tamari
Black pepper and Himalayan salt if desired (tamari tends to be salty enough on its own)

### Method:
1. In a large bowl, combine all vegetables, ginger and chili peppers.
2. In a small bowl, whisk together ingredients for the dressing.
3. Pour dressing over salad. Toss. Sprinkle sesame seeds over salad. Serve.

## Health-Kick Beet Salad

*Tasty, healthy, colorful and simple, this is a satisfying salad to complement any meal. This recipe is equally delicious with red or golden beets.*

### Ingredients:
*Makes approximately 4 servings*

6 red or golden beets
Beet greens, finely chopped, if desired
⅓ cup (80 ml) fresh parsley, chopped
1 clove of garlic, minced

1 teaspoon (5 ml) oregano
1 tablespoon (15 ml) balsamic vinegar
2 tablespoons (30 ml) olive oil
Himalayan salt and black pepper to taste

### Method:
1. Peel beets and chop them into chunks of desired size and thickness.
2. Place in a large pot and cover with water. Bring to a bowl. Reduce heat and simmer for about 10 to 15 minutes, or until beets are soft. Drain and let beets cool thoroughly.
3. Place beets in a large bowl and add all other ingredients. Toss gently. Serve at room temperature or chilled.

*"Before you taste anything, recite a blessing." ~Rabbi Akiva*

# The Josephine: A Tahini Dressing

*I have a little challenge going on called **"Veganize This!"** Whenever someone asks me for a vegan version of something they love, I get to work veganizing, and then name the dish after them. This is for Josephine, a former student of my vegan cooking course at McGill University. She asked me if I could think up a vegan dressing containing tahini and ginger. Thank you for this yummy inspiration, Josephine!*

### Ingredients:
*Makes approximately 2 servings*

1 cup (250 ml) quinoa
1 ½ cups (375 ml) water
2 cups (500 ml) raw kale or lettuce of your choice

### Dressing:
2 tablespoons (30 ml) tahini
2 tablespoons (30 ml) olive oil
2 tablespoons (30 ml) balsamic vinegar
1 tablespoon (15 ml) wheat-free tamari
½ teaspoon (2.5 ml) Himalayan salt
1 tablespoon (15 ml) oregano
1 clove of garlic, finely minced
1 small piece of ginger, finely minced

### Topping:
5 dried apricots or 2 fresh apricots, finely chopped
1 tablespoon (15 ml) chia seeds
1 tablespoon (15 ml) ground flaxseed
1 tablespoon (15 ml) hemp seeds

### Method:
1. Place quinoa and water in a pot and bring to a boil. Lower heat and simmer, covered, until all water has been absorbed, about 10 to 15 minutes. Remove from heat and set aside to cool.
2. In a small bowl, whisk ingredients for the dressing.
3. In a large bowl or plate, place cooled quinoa on a bed of raw kale or any lettuce you desire. Drizzle dressing, sprinkle seeds and pieces of apricot over top. Serve.

# La Mexicana: Cilantro Salad

*A cilantro salad? Is this a Mexican-style tabbouleh? Fun! Instead of parsley, use cilantro. Instead of lemon, try lime. Add cherry tomatoes and avocado. Instead of couscous, how about we try quinoa? And there we have it: La Mexicana, an ode to my beloved Mexico.*

**Ingredients:**
*Makes approximately 3 to 4 servings*

½ cup (125 ml) quinoa, cooked and cooled (sprouted if desired)
3 cups (750 ml) fresh cilantro, finely chopped
7 or 8 cherry tomatoes, quartered
1 small avocado, chopped
5 to 6 green onions, finely chopped
½ cup (125 ml) lime juice, freshly squeezed
2 tablespoons (30 ml) olive oil
1 garlic clove, minced
1 teaspoon (5 ml) Himalayan salt
½ teaspoon (2.5 ml) chili flakes
¼ teaspoon (1.25 ml) black pepper, freshly ground
3 tablespoons (45 ml) hemp seeds

**Method:**
1. Toss ingredients, except hemp seeds, in a large bowl. Garnish with hemp seeds and serve.

*"Life is life - whether in a cat, or dog or man. There is no difference there between a cat or a man. The idea of difference is a human conception for man's own advantage."* ~Sri Aurobindo

## Yin-Yang Counterbalance: Mango Avocado Salad

*The flavors of avocado and mango are very complementary. In Chinese medicine, the mango is said to be rich in wood energy, a yang male force, whereas the avocado is considered a yin earth element, female food. Savor the bliss of this dish's yin-yang balance!*

### Ingredients:
*Makes approximately 2 servings*

2 mangos, chopped
1 small tomato, chopped
½ small red onion, chopped
2 tablespoons (30 ml) olive oil
Juice from one lime
1 avocado, chopped

1 clove of garlic, minced
2 cups (500 ml) baby spinach
1 teaspoon (5 ml) hemp seeds, shelled
1 teaspoon (5 ml) red chili flakes
1 tablespoon (15 ml) fresh parsley, finely chopped
Himalayan salt and black pepper to taste

### Method:
1. Combine chopped mango, tomato and onion in a small bowl. Add one tablespoon (15 ml) olive oil, ½ the amount of lime juice and salt. Stir.
2. Combine chopped avocado and minced garlic in a separate bowl. Add one tablespoon (15 ml) olive oil, the remaining lime juice and salt. Stir.
3. On a large flat dish, place bed of spinach leaves.
4. Arrange mango mixture and avocado mixture in a yin-yang formation over spinach. Sprinkle black pepper, hemp seeds, chili flakes and parsley over top. Serve at room temperature or chilled.

# Two Coleslaws: Spicy Italian and Creamy Classic

*As with Italian potato salad, Italian Coleslaw is not made with mayonnaise. We use olive oil and white vinegar instead. However, if you prefer the creamy classic-style with mayonnaise, I offer you my vegan version as an alternative dressing. Here is the creamy one in the picture above. It's absolutely irresistible!*

**Ingredients:**
*Makes approximately 4 to 6 servings*

1 small green cabbage, shredded
4 small carrots, peeled and shredded
1 medium red onion, finely chopped

**Spicy Italian coleslaw dressing**
1 or 2 garlic cloves, minced
3 red chili peppers, finely chopped
3 tablespoons (45 ml) olive oil
1 teaspoon (5 ml) black pepper
⅓ cup (80 ml) white vinegar

**Creamy Classic coleslaw dressing**
¾ cup (180 ml) vegan mayonnaise
1 tablespoon (15 ml) Dijon mustard
1 tablespoon (15 ml) lemon juice
1 tablespoon (15 ml) apple cider vinegar
2 teaspoons (10 ml) Himalayan salt
1 teaspoon (5 ml) black pepper

**Method:**
1. Combine shredded cabbage, carrots and onions in a large bowl.
2. In a small bowl, combine your choice of dressing ingredients. Whisk.
3. Pour vinaigrette over cabbage, toss and serve.

*"I salute the light within your eyes where the whole universe dwells. For when you are at that center within you and I am at that place within me, we shall be one." ~Chief Crazy Horse*

## Lemon Lime Bean Medley Salad

*An array of flavors and colors, this salad satisfies the eyes as much as the palate. Fresh, yet very filling, this is definitely a "main dish"- type salad.*

### Ingredients:
*Makes approximately 3 to 4 servings*

4 carrots, peeled
3 black radishes, peeled (or 1 daikon, peeled)
1 small piece of ginger, peeled
1 cup (250 ml) cooked lentils, cooled
1 cup (250 ml) cooked beans, any variety, cooled
1 small red onion, thinly sliced
1 clove of garlic, minced

1 celery stalk, finely chopped
Juice from one lemon and one lime
3 tablespoons (45 ml) flaxseed oil
2 teaspoons (10 ml) Himalayan salt
¼ teaspoon (1.25 ml) cayenne pepper
½ cup (125 ml) fresh parsley, chopped
2 tablespoons (30 ml) shelled hemp seeds

### Method:
1. Shred carrots, black radish (or daikon) and ginger in a food processor.
2. Combine all ingredients, except the hemp seeds and parsley, in a large bowl. Mix well. Garnish with chopped parsley and hemp seeds.

## Creamy Cashew Onion Dip

*Looking for a dairy-free, sour cream-like dipping experience? Look no further – even vegans can dip! I wanted to create a creamy vegan onion dip for chips and veggies to completely dazzle your guests and I think I succeeded. I personally love hot peppers, but the jalapeño is entirely optional here. Adding an avocado to this recipe is a very tasty alternative, making it even creamier and more delicious!*

**Ingredients:**
Makes approximately 6 to 8 servings

1 cup (250 ml) raw cashews, soaked overnight
½ cup (125 ml) water
2 tablespoons (30 ml) olive oil
2 teaspoons (10 ml) lemon juice
4 tablespoons (60 ml) nutritional yeast
½ teaspoon (2.5 ml) red chili flakes
2 cloves of garlic, minced
¼ cup (60 ml) fresh parsley, chopped
2 teaspoons (10 ml) Himalayan salt
1 avocado, mashed (optional)
½ teaspoon (2.5 ml) black pepper
1 tablespoon (15 ml) dried chives
⅓ cup (80 ml) green onion, finely chopped
¼ cup (60 ml) fresh dill, chopped
¼ cup (60 ml) fresh parsley, chopped
1 jalapeño pepper, thinly sliced (optional)

**Method:**
1. Drain cashews and place in a blender or food processor. Add water, oil, lemon juice, nutritional yeast, chili flakes, garlic, parsley and salt. Add the optional mashed avocado, if desired. Blend until creamy.
2. Pour into bowl. Add remaining ingredients and stir. Garnish with added chives, small pieces of green onion and jalapeño pepper, if desired.
3. Chill for at least 3 hours in the refrigerator to allow all the flavors to blend perfectly. If you can, make this dip the day before and let the flavors marinate in the fridge overnight. Serve with veggies, crackers or your choice of chips.

*"The real voyage of discovery is not in seeking new landscapes but in having new eyes."*
~Marcel Proust

## Kale Goji Berry "Rocket Fuel" Salad

*Do you want to "fly to the moon" with energy and vibrancy? Then this salad is for you, as it's teeming with superfoods! If you use the tamari, no added salt is needed since the tamari provides sufficient saltiness.*

**Ingredients:**
*Makes approximately 2 to 3 servings*

2 to 3 cups (500-750 ml) curly kale, stems removed and chopped
1 cup (250 ml) broccoli, chopped, blanched and cooled
1 tablespoon (15 ml) goji berries, pre-soaked for 15 minutes
1 tablespoon (15 ml) shelled hemp seeds
1 tablespoon (15 ml) ground flaxseed
1 teaspoon (5 ml) chia seeds
1 or 2 tablespoons (15 -30 ml) wheat-free tamari or balsamic vinegar
1 or 2 tablespoons (15-30 ml) olive oil or flaxseed oil
Almond shavings

**Method:**
1. Toss all ingredients in a large bowl. Sprinkle almond shavings on top if desired. Serve.

## Basil Artichoke Spread

*Artichoke hearts, when combined in this spread with basil, have an elegant and sophisticated flavor. This recipe is excellent as an appetizer on crackers or your favorite bread.*

**Ingredients:**
*Makes approximately 4 servings*

1 ½ cups (375 ml) artichoke hearts, boiled and cooled
3 large fresh basil leaves, chopped
1 clove of garlic, minced
¼ cup (60 ml) nutritional yeast
Juice from ½ a lemon
2 tablespoons (30 ml) olive oil
2 tablespoons (30 ml) water
1 teaspoon (5 ml) black pepper
1 teaspoon (5 ml) chili flakes
Himalayan salt if required (if using canned artichokes, they are already cooked and salted)

**Method:**
1. Combine all ingredients in a food processor or blender and blend until creamy.
2. Garnish with fresh basil, if desired. Serve as a spread or dip. Excellent in a sandwich with arugula lettuce.

*"A man can live and be healthy without killing animals for food; therefore, if he eats meat, he participates in taking animal life merely for the sake of his appetite. And to act so is immoral."*
*~Leo Tolstoy*

# Baba Maria Ganoush

*I just adore eggplants – it's in my Italian blood! I find this recipe so delicious it brings tears to my eyes every time! As you know, we should avoid olive oil in cooked recipes, but for this one, the flavor is essential to the recipe. You can, however, substitute olive oil for any oil you prefer, so long as you don't mind the slight alteration to the taste.*

### Ingredients:
*Makes approximately 4 to 5 servings*

1 large eggplant
2 tablespoons (30 ml) olive oil
1 or 2 cloves of garlic, minced
¼ cup (60 ml) tahini
⅓ cup (80 ml) water
2 tablespoons (30 ml) lemon juice
½ teaspoon (2.5 ml) red chili flakes
½ teaspoon (2.5 ml) cumin
½ teaspoon (2.5 ml) paprika
1 teaspoon (5 ml) Himalayan salt, or more to taste
2 tablespoons (30 ml) fresh parsley

### Method:
1. Preheat oven to 375°F (190°C).
2. Slice eggplant in half horizontally. Rub a small amount of olive oil on the inside halves and place face down on a cooking sheet or large casserole dish. Bake for 45 minutes or until very soft.
3. Remove from oven and let cool. Once cool, remove skin with your fingers and discard. Place eggplant in a colander and allow excess liquid to drain. (Leave it in the colander for about 30 minutes.)
4. Place eggplant in a large bowl and add all remaining ingredients and stir. Place mixture in a blender or food processor and blend until soft. If your mixture is too thick, you may add more water. Taste test to see if you need more salt.
5. Place in a small serving bowl. You may sprinkle more paprika, drizzle olive oil on top if you desire and garnish with chopped parsley. Baba ganoush is lovely with Kalamata or Moroccan olives and pita.

### Maria's Guacamole

*So delicious, so nutritious and so many wonderful ways to serve it, guacamole is a crowd pleaser every time. For my guacamole recipe, I like to keep it really simple and focus on the superb taste of avocadoes. I love it on my Portobello Mushroom Burger (see page 90 for recipe).*

**Ingredients:**
*Makes approximately 2 to 4 servings*

2 ripe avocados
3 green onions or ½ white onion, finely chopped
1 clove of garlic, minced
1 small tomato, diced

Juice from one lime
½ teaspoon (2.5 ml) Himalayan salt
½ teaspoon (2.5 ml) black pepper
Chili flakes (optional)

**Method:**
1. Scoop out avocados and mash with a fork or masher in a small bowl.
2. Add in all other ingredients and mix well. Serve immediately or chilled.

*"You cannot teach a man anything; you can only help him find it within himself." ~Galielo Galilei*

## Arabian Mint Lentil Salad

*The subtle mint, lemon and cumin flavors in combination add a mystical, exotic excitement to this salad.*
*A culinary delight and very satisfying, it can easily be the centerpiece main dish.*

**Ingredients:**
*Makes approximately 5 to 6 servings*

2 cups (500 ml) green lentils
5 cups (1 ¼ L) water
2 tablespoons (30 ml) grapeseed oil
5 cloves of garlic, finely minced
¼ cup (60 ml) lemon juice (1 or 2 lemons)
and lemon zest from one lemon
½ teaspoon (2.5 ml) chili flakes
2 tablespoons (30 ml) olive oil
½ teaspoon (2.5 ml) cumin
½ cup (125 ml) fresh parsley, chopped
¼ cup (60 ml) fresh mint, chopped
½ white onion, thinly sliced
Himalayan salt and black pepper to taste

**Method:**
1. Place lentils in a pot with water and bring to a boil. Lower heat and let simmer, partially covered, until lentils are soft, about 45 minutes to 1 hour. (Green lentils usually take a little longer to cook than other lentils.) When lentils are soft, water will most likely have been fully absorbed. If not, drain excess water. Set lentils aside to cool.
2. In a frying pan, heat grapeseed oil and add garlic. Sauté until slightly golden, about 3 minutes. Turn off heat and set aside to cool.
3. In a blender, add lemon juice and zest, chili flakes, olive oil, cumin, cooled garlic and oil. Blend briefly.
4. Place cooled lentils in a large bowl. Pour dressing from the blender over lentils. Add chopped parsley, mint and onion. Mix well. Add salt and black pepper to taste. Serve at room temperature or chilled. Garnish with additional lemon zest and mint leaves, if desired.

# El Tabbouleh Loco

*I call this tabbouleh "loco" (crazy) because I kicked the "hotness" up a few notches by adding ginger and red chili peppers! This tabbouleh is on fire! It may be too hot for you, and if it is, leave out one of these ingredients or both. I also heightened its nutritional value by including quinoa and flaxseed oil. I recommend using flat-leaf parsley because it has more flavor.*

### Ingredients:
*Makes approximately 4 servings*

3 cups (750 ml) fresh parsley, chopped
½ cup (125 ml) quinoa, cooked
4 green onions, chopped
1 small tomato, chopped
1 tablespoon (15 ml) fresh ginger, minced
2 cloves of garlic, minced
1 red chili pepper, chopped
Juice from one lemon
1 tablespoon (15 ml) flaxseed oil
1 tablespoon (15 ml) olive oil
1 teaspoon (5 ml) Himalayan salt

### Method:
1. Combine all ingredients in a large bowl and toss. Serve chilled or at room temperature.

*"Why should man expect his prayer for mercy to be heard by what is above him when he shows no mercy to what is under him?" ~Pierre Troubetzkoy*

## A Taste of Autumn Salad

*If autumn has a taste, it tastes like this. This salad even looks like autumn to me with the hint of green from the fennel, a soft brown from the walnuts and red speckles from the cranberries. It's lovely as is, or can be served on a bed of cooled quinoa.*

**Ingredients:**
*Makes approximately 2 servings*

1 fennel bulb, core removed and thinly sliced
1 Bosc pear, sliced
Handful of dried cranberries
Handful of raw walnuts
2 tablespoons (30 ml) flaxseed oil
Juice from one lime or one lemon
Himalayan salt and freshly ground black pepper to taste

**Method:**
1. Toss all ingredients in a large bowl.
2. Serve on its own, or on a bed of cooled quinoa.

## Parma-Sprinkled Bruschetta

*As an appetizer or to accompany almost any dish, this tasty tomato appetizer is a favorite for many and can be served on any type of bread, although baguette-type bread is common. Crackers or even raw daikon slices can work too!*

### Ingredients:
Makes 4 to 6 servings

5 ripe tomatoes
½ cup (125 ml) fresh parsley, stems removed, chopped
3 cloves of garlic, minced
2 tablespoons (30 ml) olive oil
1 teaspoon (5 ml) Himalayan salt
1 tablespoon (15 ml) lemon juice
¼ teaspoon (1.25 ml) black pepper
1 whole wheat baguette, sliced into maximum one- inch thick (2 cm) slices
1 teaspoon (5 ml) Himalayan salt
Vegan parmesan for topping (see recipe on page 39)

### Method:
1. Preheat oven to 375°F (190°C).
2. Dice tomatoes and place in a large bowl. Mix in chopped parsley, garlic, olive oil, salt, lemon juice and black pepper.
3. Slice your baguette into thin slices and lay in single layer on a baking sheet. Bake for 5 minutes.
4. Remove from the oven. Top each slice of bread with approximately 1 tablespoon of tomato mixture. Return to the oven and bake for another 5 minutes. Remove from oven.
5. Sprinkle vegan parmesan over bruschetta and serve warm.

*"The most powerful agent of growth and transformation is something much more basic than any technique: a change of heart." ~John Welwood*

## Immune-Boosting Raw Garnish

*How do we support our immune system through diet? By choosing unprocessed plant-based foods rich in vitamins, zinc, beta-carotene, powerful antioxidants, and foods with natural antibacterial, antiseptic and antiviral properties. Add this tasty little raw concoction to soups and main dishes and give your immune system a boost!*

**Ingredients:**

2 to 3 red and green hot peppers of your choice, chopped
1 cup (250 ml) fresh parsley, chopped
1 white onion, chopped
1 to 2 cloves of garlic, minced
2 tablespoons (30 ml) fresh ginger, minced
Pinch Himalayan salt

**Method:**

1. Mix all these ingredients in a small bowl. Add a pinch of salt. Use as a garnish over everything!

Fully Plant-Based
Main Meals and Side Dishes

# A Vegan's Shepherd's Pie with Cashew-Creamed Corn

*This is a very tasty, satisfying meal that is sure to please the whole family. This recipe works equally well with beans or tofu. Make a batch on the weekend, and enjoy the ease of heating up leftovers during the week. If you choose beans, see page 17 for soaking and cooking tips.*

### Ingredients:
Makes approximately 6 servings

1 package (454 g) organic firm tofu or 2 cups (500 ml) kidney or black beans (cooked), marinated as per recipe which follows
5 medium potatoes, chopped
1 medium sweet potato, chopped
1 ½ teaspoons (7.5 ml) Himalayan salt
1 clove garlic
1 tablespoon (15 ml) nutritional yeast
2 tablespoons (30 ml) vegan butter
2 tablespoons (30 ml) grapeseed oil

1 white onion, chopped
2 cups (500 ml) mushrooms, chopped
2 cups (500 ml) spinach, chopped
3 cups (750 ml) organic corn, preferably frozen corn, cooked
1 cup (250 ml) cashew-creamed corn (recipe follows)
2 teaspoons (10 ml) paprika or ½ teaspoon (2.5 ml) cayenne pepper

### Method:
1. Marinate tofu or cooked beans according to the recipe below and refrigerate overnight or for several hours.
2. Boil potatoes and sweet potato in water with salt and garlic until pieces are soft (20 to 30 minutes). Once cooked, drain potatoes, add nutritional yeast and butter and mash with a potato masher. Set aside.
3. Add grapeseed oil to pan and heat. Add marinated tofu or beans, onion and mushrooms. Sauté at low to medium heat for about 20 minutes. Add spinach. Continue cooking for 2 more minutes.
4. Place cooked tofu or beans, mushrooms and spinach as bottom layer in a large rectangular glass casserole dish.
5. Add corn and cashew-creamed corn (recipe follows) as second layer.
6. Add mashed potatoes as top layer, spreading evenly with a fork. Sprinkle paprika or cayenne pepper on top.
7. Place casserole dish in oven and bake at 350°F (180°C) for 10 to 15 minutes. You may set your oven to broil for a couple of minutes as well. Serve warm.

*How to Marinate Tofu or Beans:*

Cut the slab of tofu into thick slices and place on a plate lined with paper towels to absorb excess liquid. Cover tofu with more paper towels. Use a plate as a compress. Let the tofu sit for about 20 minutes. In a large glass container, place tofu (crumbled for Shepherd's Pie or chopped for other recipes) or beans, and mix in the ingredients which follow. Refrigerate overnight or for at least 4 hours prior to cooking.

2 cloves of garlic, minced
3 tablespoons (45 ml) olive or grapeseed oil
1 teaspoon (5 ml) fennel seeds
2 tablespoons (30 ml) unsalted steak spice (see my homemade steak spice blend on page 69)
1 teaspoon (5 ml) oregano

3 tablespoons (45 ml) fresh parsley, minced
½ teaspoon (2.5 ml) ground black pepper
2 tablespoons (30 ml) balsamic vinegar
2 tablespoons (30 ml) wheat-free tamari
1 bay leaf

*Cashew-Creamed Corn*
**Ingredients:**

½ cup (125 ml) raw cashews, pre-soaked for 2 hours, drained
1 cup (250 ml) water
1 garlic, minced
½ teaspoon (2.5 ml) Himalayan salt
2 tablespoons (30 ml) tahini
2 tablespoons (30 ml) olive oil

¼ cup (60 ml) shelled hemp seeds
¼ cup (60 ml) nutritional yeast
½ teaspoon (2.5 ml) black pepper
1 cup (250 ml) corn, cooked (¾ cups (180 ml) for blending in a blender and ¼ cup (60 ml) to be set aside and added to the blended corn)

**Method:**
1. Blend all ingredients until creamy in blender. Add ¼ cup (60 ml) corn, which had been set aside, to creamy mixture and stir.
2. Add to shepherd's pie or other recipes.

*"Start a huge, foolish project, like Noah. It makes absolutely no difference what people think of you."*
*~Rumi*

## Tofu Mex Scramble

*This colorful and tasty tofu scramble is inspired by kindness and again, some of my favorite tastes from Mexico. It's fantastic served with a few slices of tomato and avocado.*

### Ingredients:
*Makes approximately 4 servings*

1 package (454 g) organic firm tofu
2 tablespoons (30 ml) grapeseed oil
5 green onions, chopped
1 clove of garlic, minced
1 small red bell pepper, finely chopped
1 jalapeño pepper, finely chopped (optional)
2 ½ teaspoons (12.5 ml) Himalayan salt, more if desired
½ teaspoon (2.5 ml) cumin
½ cup (125 ml) black beans, cooked and drained (see "Soaking and Cooking Beans" section on page 17)
Handful of baby spinach
1 teaspoon (5 ml) turmeric
¼ cup (60 ml) fresh cilantro, chopped
Freshly ground black pepper

### Method:
1. Cut the tofu slab into thick slices and place on a plate lined with paper towels to absorb excess liquid. Cover tofu with more paper towels. Use a plate as a compress. Let the tofu sit for about 20 minutes.
2. Using your fingers or a fork, crumble tofu.
3. Heat oil in a large skillet over medium heat. Add onion, garlic, peppers and a teaspoon (5 ml) of salt and sauté, stirring occasionally, until soft, about 4 to 5 minutes.
4. Stir in tofu, rest of the salt and cumin. Cook for 5 minutes, stirring often. Add beans, spinach and turmeric. Cook, stirring often, for about 2 minutes.
5. Remove from heat. Stir in chopped cilantro. Add more salt if desired and black pepper to taste. Serve warm with chopped cherry tomatoes, avocado, warm tortillas or toast, if desired.

## Felicia's Eggplant No-Parmigiana

*This is a classic Italian dish, minus the parmesan cheese. I find it tastes just as good without it, but you are always welcome to add my vegan parmesan if you so desire (see page 39 for recipe). My sister always loved this classic Italian dish growing up, and now she loves it even more since I veganized it. I love her, so this one's for her, and for you too of course! Enjoy!*

**Ingredients:**
*Makes approximately 4 to 5 servings*
2 large eggplants
½ cup (125 ml) grapeseed oil
2 teaspoons (10 ml) Himalayan salt
2 cups (500 ml) Basil Tomato Sauce (see recipe on page 76)
1 cup (250 ml) fresh parsley, chopped
4 fresh basil leaves
1 tablespoon (15 ml) hemp seeds
Freshly ground black pepper to taste

**Method:**
1. Slice eggplants into thin, round pieces.
2. Arrange slices layer by layer in a colander, sprinkling salt over each layer. Cover colander with a plate and place a weight over the plate to apply pressure to the slices of eggplant. This will help drain excess water from the eggplant. Let drain for 4 to 5 hours before cooking. As you remove slices of eggplant from the colander, gently squeeze out any remaining moisture.
3. Preheat oven to 350°F (180°C).
4. In a large saucepan on your stovetop, heat the oil at high heat. Introduce 4 to 5 slices of eggplant (as many as could fit in the pan without crowding) and fry for about 3 or 4 minutes, or until they appear slightly golden. Turn pieces over and repeat. Once cooked, place each slice of eggplant on paper towels to drain excess oil.
5. In a large glass casserole dish, add one cup (250 ml) of tomato sauce. Place pieces of cooked eggplant in casserole and once layer is complete, add sauce to the whole layer. Start another layer with pieces of cooked eggplant and repeat procedures until all eggplant pieces are in the casserole. Place casserole in the oven and bake for 10 minutes.
6. Remove from oven and garnish with parsley, basil leaves, hemp seeds and pepper, if desired. Serve warm. You may also wish to sprinkle vegan parmesan over the eggplant (see recipe on page 39).

*"Be the change that you want to see in the world."* ~Mahatma Gandhi

## Rapini Mushroom Black Bean Pilaf

*There are not many things that I love more than rapini. With a pungent and slightly bitter taste, this leafy green is a common favorite in Italian cuisine. Make it in this recipe with quinoa, or try rapini with pasta in one of my favorite Italian classics: pasta "aglio e olio". "Aglio e olio" means "garlic and oil" and is an irresistible sauce for spaghetti (or any pasta you like) with rapini and/or mushrooms. If rapini is out of your comfort zone, use spinach, Swiss chard or kale, each of which can be prepared in a similar fashion.*

### Ingredients:
*Makes approximately 2 servings*

1 cup (250 ml) quinoa
1 ½ (375 ml) cups water
4 tablespoons (60 ml) grapeseed oil
5 cloves of garlic, minced
1 teaspoon (5 ml) red chili flakes
Bunch of rapini, stems removed, chopped
1 cup (250 ml) mushrooms, chopped

½ cup (125 ml) black beans, cooked
1 tablespoon (15 ml) oregano
1 tablespoon (15 ml) olive oil
3 green onions, chopped
Juice from one lemon
Himalayan salt to taste

### Method:
1. In a large sauce pan, toast quinoa for 3 to 4 minutes over medium heat. Add water and cover. When it begins to boil, lower heat to simmer. Simmer (covered) until all water is absorbed, stirring occasionally, about 10 minutes. Remove from heat and set aside.
2. In a large pot, heat 2 tablespoons (30 ml) of grapeseed oil over medium heat. Add 3 cloves of minced garlic, and 1 teaspoon (5 ml) chili flakes. Sauté until garlic is golden, about 2 minutes. Add chopped rapini and 1 teaspoon (5 ml) of salt. Sauté uncovered until rapini is soft, about 8 to 10 minutes. Set aside.
3. In a sauce pan, heat remaining grapeseed oil and add 1 minced garlic. Add chopped mushrooms and a pinch of salt. Sauté until mushrooms are soft, about 4 minutes.
4. In a large bowl, combine cooked black beans, quinoa, oregano, olive oil, remaining garlic, chopped green onions and lemon juice. Add more salt to taste.
5. Serve rapini and mushrooms warm on top of quinoa and black bean bed.

# Brown Basmati and Long Grain Wild Rice with Green Veggies

*This rice and vegetable combo goes superbly well with my bean salad (see recipe on page 33). Not only are the combined tastes superb, but together they create a nutritious, satisfying meal.*

Ingredients:
Makes approximately 5 to 6 servings

3 tablespoons (45 ml) grapeseed oil
3 to 4 cloves garlic, minced
1 cup (250 ml) long grain wild rice
1 cup (250 ml) brown basmati rice
Water or vegetable broth as required to cook rice, at least 4 cups
2 cups (500 ml) spinach, chopped
2 cups (500 ml) broccoli, chopped
1 cup (250 ml) mushrooms, chopped
1 cup (250 ml) frozen peas, boiled
2 tablespoons (30 ml) oregano
½ cup (125 ml) fresh parsley, chopped
Himalayan salt and freshly ground black pepper to taste

Method:
1. For best results, cook each type of rice separately. Each variety of rice you choose will come with specific cooking instructions due to differences in length of time required to cook. Before following those instructions, I do as follows to increase flavor (optional): heat 1 teaspoon (5 ml) of oil on low heat and 1 minced garlic for 2 to 3 minutes. Add rice and stir to allow the oil to coat the rice evenly. Add 2 cups (500 ml) of water or vegetable broth for every 1 cup (250 ml) of rice. Add approximately 1 teaspoon (5 ml) of salt. Cover and let simmer. Stir frequently.
2. Once all the liquid is absorbed, taste the rice to see if the desired consistency has been reached. If it is still too hard, add a little more liquid and repeat taste test once all liquid is absorbed.
3. While rice is cooking, sauté vegetables with garlic, salt and oil. Again, for best results, cook the vegetables separately.
4. Place peas in a pot with 2 cups (500 ml) of water and bring to a boil. Once water boils, immediately remove from heat and drain. Set aside.
5. Once rice is cooked and vegetables are ready, combine all ingredients in a large serving bowl. Add oregano. Taste test to determine if more salt is required. Add pepper as desired. Garnish with chopped fresh parsley. Serve warm.

*"Your life must be your message." ~Thich Nhat Hanh*

## Moroccan Flair Vegan Poutine

*I veganized this classic French Canadian dish. I was inspired to heighten the poutine experience with a spice blend called,* Ras el hanout, *which gives it a distinctive Moroccan flavor. Scrumptious and simply irresistible, this dish is the ultimate feel-good meal. For the Italian poutine version, omit the* Ras el hanout, *and use my Basil Tomato Sauce (see page 76 for recipe), in place of this mushroom sauce.*

### Ingredients:
*Makes approximately 4 to 5 servings*

3 tablespoons (45 ml) Ras el Hanout (see recipe below)
1 tablespoon (15 ml) Maria's Steak Spice (see recipe below)
4 tablespoons (60 ml) grapeseed oil
2 cloves of garlic, minced
2 cups (500 ml) mushrooms, variety of your choice, chopped
1 cup (250) vegetable broth (see recipe on page 30) or water
6 white potatoes, cut into thin wedges or slices, with skin
1 teaspoon (5 ml) oregano
1 teaspoon (5 ml) fresh parsley, chopped
¾ cup (180 ml) vegan "mozzarella-style" cheese
Himalayan salt
Coconut oil or grapeseed oil for baking dish

### Method:
1. Prepare Ras el Hanout and Maria's Steak Spice.
2. To make the mushroom gravy, heat 1 tablespoon (15 ml) grapeseed oil and brown 2 cloves of minced garlic, 1 to 2 minutes. Add mushrooms, a pinch of salt and 1 tablespoon (15 ml) of Maria's Steak Spice and sauté for about 4 minutes, or until mushrooms are soft. Add vegetable broth or water and simmer for 5 minutes. Set aside to cool.
3. Preheat oven to 400°F (200°C).
4. Place potatoes in a large bowl filled with cold water. Let stand for 20 minutes.
5. Rub coconut oil or grapeseed oil on baking sheet or glass casserole dish. For those of you who do not enjoy the taste of coconut, use grapeseed oil for this step. Alternatively, you can line your baking dish with parchment paper to prevent sticking. With parchment paper, you do not need extra oil.
6. Drain potatoes and pat dry with paper towels. Transfer potatoes to clean bowl.
7. Add Ras el Hanout, 1 teaspoon (5 ml) salt, oregano and remaining grapeseed oil. Toss to combine ingredients. Arrange potato wedges in a single layer on baking sheet.

8. Bake potatoes for 25 to 30 minutes. Turn potatoes after 10 to 15 minutes. Remove from oven once crispy and golden.
9. Place mushrooms and broth in a blender. Add parsley and blend until creamy. Pour gravy over potatoes. Sprinkle shredded vegan cheese over top.

### Ras el Hanout Spice Blend

*"Ras el Hanout" means "head of the shop," implying that it's the store's best spice blend. This wonderfully aromatic spice blend is very versatile, adding an exotic touch of sweet and spicy to any dish. In a bowl, whisk all these ground spices together:*
2 teaspoons (10 ml) coriander
1 ½ teaspoons (7.5 ml) cumin
1 teaspoon (5 ml) cardamom
½ teaspoon (2.5 ml) black pepper
1 teaspoon (5 ml) turmeric
1 teaspoon (5 ml) allspice
1 teaspoon (5 ml) cinnamon
1 teaspoon (5 ml) paprika
¼ teaspoon (1.25 ml) cayenne pepper

### Maria's Steak Spice Blend

*Not crazy about the additives in some commercial steak spices on the market, I just made my own blend! All these ingredients are dried spices. Whisk together in a small bowl:*
1 ½ teaspoon (7.5 ml) onion flakes
1 ½ teaspoon (7.5 ml) granulated garlic
1 teaspoon (5 ml) oregano
1 teaspoon (5 ml) ground celery
1 teaspoon (5 ml) fennel seeds
1 teaspoon (5 ml) paprika
1 teaspoon (5 ml) coriander
½ teaspoon (2.5 ml) mustard powder
½ teaspoon (2.5 ml) ground chipotle
½ teaspoon (2.5 ml) red chili pepper flakes
½ teaspoon (2.5 ml) black pepper

## "For The Love of Chickens" Casserole with Cashew-Creamy Mushroom Sauce

*Changing our diets to appease our conscience doesn't mean giving up familiar flavors. I've said it many times: it's all about the spices. For this dish, I first made a list of the spices I associated with chicken. This is how I came up with the marinade. The tofu or cannellini beans don't have much taste on their own; they simply act like sponges to absorb any and all the flavors we want them to, so really anything is possible.*

### Ingredients:
*Makes approximately 6 servings*

1 package (454 g) organic firm tofu, chopped into large chunks or 2 cups cannellini beans, cooked
1 ½ cups (375 ml) bread crumbs (recipe follows)
2 cups (500 ml) Cashew-Creamy Mushroom Sauce (recipe follows)
3 tablespoons (45 ml) grapeseed oil
2 cloves of garlic, minced
1 head of broccoli, chopped
1 head of cauliflower, chopped
1 celery stalk, chopped
2 cups (500 ml) fresh parsley, chopped
Himalayan salt and freshly ground black pepper to taste

**Ingredients for (tofu or cannellini bean) marinade**
1 ½ teaspoons (7.5 ml) Himalayan salt
½ teaspoon (2.5 ml) dried savory
½ teaspoon (2.5 ml) dried rosemary
1 teaspoon (5 ml) dried basil
½ teaspoon (2.5 ml) mustard powder
½ teaspoon (2.5 ml) paprika
½ teaspoon (2.5 ml) cumin
1 teaspoon (5 ml) thyme
½ teaspoon (2.5 ml) black pepper
¼ teaspoon (1.25 ml) cayenne pepper
2 tablespoons (30 ml) olive oil
1 to 2 cloves of garlic, crushed or minced
¼ cup (60 ml) fresh parsley, chopped

**Method:**

1. Marinate tofu or cannellini beans overnight or for several hours by placing all marinade ingredients and tofu chunks (or beans) in a glass container and refrigerate.
2. Prepare bread crumbs and Cashew-Creamy Mushroom Sauce (recipes below).
3. In a large saucepan, heat 2 tablespoons (30 ml) of grapeseed oil and minced garlic for 3 to 4 minutes over medium heat. Add chopped broccoli and cauliflower. Add salt, about ½ teaspoon (2.5 ml), and sauté for about 5 to 6 minutes or until slightly soft.
4. Lower heat slightly. Pour 1 cup (250 ml) each of mushroom sauce, bread crumbs and parsley into saucepan over vegetables. Simmer for 2 to 3 minutes.
5. Remove from heat and place into a large glass casserole dish.
6. Using the same saucepan, heat 1 tablespoon (15 ml) grapeseed oil over medium heat. Add marinated tofu or beans and chopped celery. Sauté for 10 minutes, stirring constantly. Pour 1 cup (250 ml) of mushroom sauce and ½ cup (125 ml) breadcrumbs over mixture and continue cooking for 5 more minutes, stirring constantly.
7. The sauce and bread crumbs will stick to the bottom of the pan. When you pour the tofu or bean mixture over the vegetables in the casserole dish, scrape the bottom of the pan and sprinkle roasted bread crumbs and sauce over casserole. This will add lots of flavor to the casserole. Mix vegetables and tofu (or beans) in casserole dish.
8. Garnish with more chopped fresh parsley and heat in the oven if necessary. Serve warm.

## Cashew-Creamy Mushroom Sauce

**Ingredients:**
2 tablespoons (30 ml) grapeseed oil
2 cloves of garlic, minced
3 cups (750 ml) mushrooms, chopped
½ teaspoon (2.5 ml) oregano
1 teaspoon (5 ml) Himalayan salt
½ teaspoon (2.5 ml) unsalted steak spice (see page 69 for my recipe)
½ teaspoon (2.5 ml) chili flakes
½ cup (125 ml) raw cashews, soaked for 2 hours, drained
1 ¼ (310 ml) cups water
2 tablespoons (30 ml) tahini
2 tablespoons (30 ml) olive oil
2 tablespoons (30 ml) freshly squeezed lemon juice
¼ cup (60 ml) nutritional yeast
¼ cup (60 ml) hemp seeds
½ teaspoon (2.5 ml) black pepper

**Method:**
1. In a saucepan, heat grapeseed oil and a minced garlic clove for 2 or 3 minutes on medium heat. Add mushrooms, oregano, 1 teaspoon (5 ml) salt, steak spice and chili flakes. Sauté for about 5 minutes or until mushrooms are soft. Set aside and let cool.
2. In a blender, combine drained soaked cashews, water, tahini, olive oil, lemon juice, nutritional yeast, hemp, pepper, remaining garlic and cooled mushrooms. Keep a few mushrooms on the side to add to the sauce after blending, if desired. Blend until soft and creamy. Mix in remaining mushrooms. Taste test the sauce to determine if you'd like more salt. This versatile sauce can be used for casseroles, pasta, quinoa, rice or veggie dishes.

### Homemade Bread Crumbs

**Ingredients:**
4 or 5 slices of bread of your choice, dried and hardened (takes about 2 days)
1 teaspoon (5 ml) oregano
1 teaspoon (5 ml) Himalayan salt
1 teaspoon (5 ml) garlic powder

**Method:**
1. Choose bread that you would like to grate. Break it into pieces and place on a cooking sheet. You can leave it on a countertop or in the oven for at least 2 days to dry out and harden. (Do not turn oven on!)
2. Once bread is completely dry and hard, grate it in a blender or food processor until powdery.
3. Pour into large bowl and add oregano, salt and garlic powder. Use as desired.

*"A man of my spiritual intensity does not eat corpses." ~George Bernard Shaw*

## Roasted Red Pepper and Eggplant Risotto

*A deliciously rich and creamy roasted eggplant and red pepper risotto. This dish makes for a very flavorful, colorful and satisfying main dish.*

### Ingredients:
*Makes approximately 4 servings*

2 medium red bell peppers
1 small eggplant
4 tablespoons (60 ml) grapeseed oil
1 tablespoon (15 ml) olive oil
2 cups (500 ml) long grain brown rice
4 cups (1 L) of water
2 onions, chopped
1 teaspoon (5 ml) chili flakes
4 cloves garlic, minced
2 medium tomatoes, diced
4 tablespoons (60 ml) Ras el Hanout (see recipe on page 69)
1 cup (250 ml) chickpeas, cooked (see tips in "Soaking and Cooking Beans" section on page 17)
4 tablespoons (60 ml) fresh parsley, chopped
Lemon zest from one lemon
⅓ cup (80 ml) nutritional yeast
2 tablespoons (30 ml) pine nuts
1 teaspoon (5 ml) hemp seeds, for garnish
Himalayan salt and ground black pepper to taste

### Method:
1. Preheat oven to 400°F (200°C). Slice peppers and eggplant in half and coat with grapeseed oil. Line cooking sheet with grapeseed oil and place peppers and eggplant face down. Bake for about 30 minutes to 45 minutes, uncovered, or until very soft. Remove from oven and place in colander for excess moisture to drip.
2. Heat 1 tablespoon of olive oil in a large pot over low to medium heat. Add rice and stir, allowing the oil to coat the rice. Continue stirring occasionally for about 5 minutes. Add 2 cups (500 ml) of water and cover. Once it begins boiling, reduce heat to simmer, cover and let all the water be absorbed, stirring occasionally. Add remaining 2 cups (500 ml) of water, stirring occasionally until all water is absorbed and rice is soft and sticky. Remove from heat and set aside.
3. Heat 2 tablespoons (30 ml) of grapeseed oil in a large sauce pan over medium heat. Add onions, chili flakes, garlic and a pinch of salt. Sauté until onions are soft and garlic is slightly golden. Add tomatoes and one tablespoon (15 ml) of Ras el Hanout and sauté until soft. Lower heat to simmer.
4. If the red peppers and eggplant are sufficiently cool and drained, remove the skins and discard. Cut up the flesh into small chunks.
5. Return to the sauce pan and stir in flesh from red peppers and eggplant, cooked chickpeas, parsley, lemon zest, nutritional yeast and pine nuts. Add rice and remaining Ras el Hanout. Stir thoroughly. Add salt and black pepper to taste. Remove from heat. Add hemp seeds and additional chopped parsley for garnish. Serve warm.

## Lasagna Rolls with Tofu Ricotta and Basil Tomato Sauce

*Full of rich creamy texture and flavor, everyone adores this dish! Leftovers are so good you don't even have to warm them up!*

### Ingredients:
*Makes approximately 12 to 15 rolls*

3 to 4 cups (750 ml to 1 L) Basil Tomato Sauce (recipe follows)
2 to 3 cups (500 to 750 ml) Tofu Ricotta (recipe follows)
3 tablespoons (45 ml) olive or grapeseed oil
1 large onion, chopped
4 cloves of garlic, minced
4 cups (1 L) mushrooms (your favorite or a combination of different mushrooms), chopped
3 teaspoons (15 ml) Himalayan salt
2 tablespoons (30 ml) unsalted steak spice (see page 69 for my homemade blend)
1 teaspoon (5 ml) fennel seeds
1 tablespoon (15 ml) oregano
5 cups (1 ¼ L) baby spinach, stems removed and chopped
1 package eggless, whole-wheat or rice lasagna noodles (typically about 12 to 15 lasagna noodles)
Fresh basil leaves and shelled hemp seeds for garnish

### Method:
1. Prepare Basil Tomato Sauce and Tofu Ricotta (recipes follows) and set aside.
2. Preheat oven to 350°F (180°C).
3. Heat oil in large frying pan over medium heat. Add onions and sauté until slightly soft. Add garlic and sauté for 2 to 3 minutes.
4. Add mushrooms, one teaspoon (5 ml) salt, steak spice, fennel and oregano, and sauté until mushrooms are tender, about 5 minutes. Add spinach and one teaspoon (5 ml) salt. Continue to sauté until spinach has completely wilted, about 2 minutes.
5. Remove from heat and let vegetables cool.
6. Return to the frying pan with vegetables, mix in tofu ricotta mixture (recipe follows). Pour into food processor and blend until smooth and creamy. Set aside.
7. In a large pot (or 2 pots depending on the size, lasagna noodles need lots of water to avoid breaking), add water and one teaspoon (5 ml) salt. Bring water to a boil. Cook lasagna noodles as per instructions on the box. Drain and set aside.
8. Spread one cup (250 ml) tomato sauce (recipe follows) in large glass or ceramic baking dish and add a little water to the sauce, about 3 tablespoons (45 ml).
9. Take one lasagna noodle at a time and lay it flat on a wooden cutting board. Put about 2 tablespoons (30 ml) of ricotta/vegetable mixture onto each lasagna noodle, leaving about ½ inch (1 cm) at each end uncovered.

10. Roll up each noodle tightly and place it seam-side-down in sauce-covered baking dish.
11. Once all lasagna rolls are placed in the baking dish, pour remaining sauce over them.
12. Cover dish with aluminum foil. Perforate foil in a few places to allow steam to escape. Bake for 30 to 40 minutes.
13. Remove from oven and garnish with fresh basil and hemp seeds. Serve warm.

## Tofu Ricotta

**Ingredients:**

1 package (454 g) organic firm tofu, drained and cut into quarters or crumbled
1 cup (250 ml) water
½ cup (125 ml) tahini
¼ cup (60 ml) olive oil
4 garlic cloves, minced
2 teaspoons (10 ml) fresh basil, chopped
1 teaspoon (5 ml) oregano
1 teaspoon (5 ml) salt

**Method:**
1. Blend all ingredients in a food processor until smooth and creamy.

## Basil Tomato Sauce

**Ingredients:**
*Makes about 4 cups (1 L) of sauce*
3 tablespoons (45 ml) olive or grapeseed oil
2 onions, chopped
1 red bell pepper, chopped
4 cloves of garlic, minced
4 cups (1 L) strained tomatoes (variety that is sold in a glass jar)
⅓ cup (80 ml) tomato paste (optional if you like really thick sauce)
1 bay leaf
3 tablespoons (45 ml) fresh parsley, chopped
6 leaves fresh basil
Himalayan salt to taste

**Method:**
1. Heat oil in large pot. Add chopped onions and pepper, and sauté for 5 minutes. Add garlic and sauté for 2 to 3 minutes.
2. Stir in all remaining ingredients and let simmer for 1 ½ to 2 hours, stirring occasionally. Discard bay leaf and basil leaves before serving.

*"Eyes are blind. You have to look with the heart." ~Antoine de Saint-Exupéry*

## Lina's Polpette: No-Meatballs

*I grew up to the smell of tomato sauce and "polpette" slowly cooking on the stovetop every Sunday morning. Those were the first irresistible aromas, sizzling sounds and bright colors that seduced me into the completely mesmerizing world of cooking. This recipe is for the one who ignited my love affair with the kitchen: my mother, Lina.*

**Ingredients:**
*Makes approximately 15 to 20 polpette*

Basil Tomato Sauce (see recipe on page 76)
1 package (454 g) organic firm tofu
1 cup (250 ml) chickpeas, kidney or cannellini beans, cooked (see tips in the section "Soaking and Cooking Beans" on page 17) and marinated (see marinade below)
5 tablespoons (75 ml) ground flaxseed
½ cup (125 ml) water
3 tablespoons (45 ml) grapeseed oil
1 onion, finely chopped
4 cloves of garlic, minced
1 red pepper, finely chopped
1 small potato, peeled and finely chopped
1 beet or 2 small carrots, peeled and finely chopped
1 cup (250 ml) mushrooms, finely chopped
1 celery stalk, finely chopped
1 zucchini, finely chopped

4 teaspoons (20 ml) Himalayan salt
½ teaspoon (2.5 ml) black pepper
1 teaspoon (5 ml) oregano
1 teaspoon (5 ml) fennel seeds
1 cup (250 ml) fresh parsley, finely chopped
1 teaspoon (5 ml) paprika
1 teaspoon (5 ml) ground chipotle
1 teaspoon (5 ml) turmeric
½ teaspoon (2.5 ml) cumin
2 ½ cups (625 ml) chickpea flour
4 teaspoons (20 ml) egg replacer
½ cup (125 ml) shelled hemp seeds
½ cup (125 ml) nutritional yeast
2 cups (500 ml) bread crumbs (see recipe on page 93)
½ cup (125 ml) water

**Method:**
1. Prepare Basil Tomato Sauce (see recipe on page 76).
2. Marinate tofu and beans (see recipe below).
3. In a small bowl, mix ground flaxseed and ½ cup (125 ml) of water. Set aside for 20 minutes.
4. Heat grapeseed oil in large frying pan. Add onions, garlic, and all chopped vegetables. Add salt, pepper, oregano and fennel seeds. Sauté until vegetables are soft, about 10 to 15 minutes.
5. Add marinated tofu and beans to vegetable mixture and stir. Cook for 5 minutes. Stir in chopped parsley, paprika, chipotle, turmeric and cumin.

6. Remove from heat and let cool. Transfer to a large bowl and stir in 1 ½ (375 ml) cups chickpea flour, egg replacer, hemp, nutritional yeast and bread crumbs. Place ½ of the mixture into food processor. Add ½ cup (125 ml) of water and blend until soft and clumpy.
7. Add blended mixture back to bowl with vegetables. Stir in flaxseed mixture. Add remaining chickpea flour. Stir well. Mixture will be very sticky.
8. Form the balls with your hands and coat with bread crumbs. You can add them to your pot of tomato sauce and allow them to simmer for 30 to 45 minutes in the sauce, gently stirring occasionally.
9. Alternatively, if you prefer to bake them, you can add about 1 cup (250 ml) of tomato sauce to a casserole dish, place the polpette in the casserole, and cover each polpette with sauce. Bake them (covered with aluminum foil, perforated with a fork to allow steam to escape) at 350°F (180°C) for 40 to 50 minutes. Gently turn the polpette over after 20 minutes of baking, and then return them to the oven for the remaining time.
10. Serve warm with pasta or salad, or any way you desire!

### Marinade for Tofu and Beans/Chickpeas

Before marinating tofu, cut the tofu slab into thick slices and place on a plate lined with paper towels to absorb excess liquid. Cover tofu with more paper towels. Use a plate as a compress. Let the tofu sit for about 20 minutes.

In a large glass container, place crumbled tofu and beans (or chickpeas). Mix in the ingredients which follow. Marinate for about 2 hours prior to cooking.
2 cloves of garlic, minced
3 tablespoons (45 ml) olive or grapeseed oil
2 tablespoons (30 ml) unsalted steak spice (see my homemade blend recipe on page 69)
3 tablespoons (45 ml) fresh parsley, minced
½ teaspoon (2.5 ml) ground black pepper
2 tablespoons (30 ml) balsamic vinegar
2 tablespoons (30 ml) wheat-free tamari
1 bay leaf (remove before cooking)

## Green Vegetable Sesame Risotto

*A successful risotto has to be creamy, but it doesn't have to contain any dairy products. Indulge yourself in this luxuriously rich and exquisite dish. I chose to use brown basmati rice for its high nutritional value, but you can use another type of rice if you prefer.*

**Ingredients:**
*Makes approximately 5 to 6 servings*

3 tablespoons (45 ml) olive oil
3 cloves garlic, minced
2 cups (500 ml) brown basmati rice
4 cups (1 L) water (or 2 cups (500 ml) vegetable broth and 2 cups (500 ml) water)
⅓ cup (80 ml) tahini
3 tablespoons (45 ml) sesame seeds (you can mix in black sesame seeds as well)
⅓ cup (80 ml) nutritional yeast
2 cups (500 ml) zucchini, chopped
1 teaspoon (5 ml) oregano
1 ½ cups (375 ml) green Cuban pepper

2 cups (500 ml) mushrooms, chopped
4 cups (1 L) Swiss chard or spinach, chopped
1 cup (250 ml) fresh parsley, chopped
Himalayan salt and black pepper to taste

**Method:**
1. In a large pot, heat 1 tablespoon (15 ml) of olive oil and 1 clove of minced garlic. Sauté on low heat for 3 to 4 minutes. Add rice and stir, allowing the rice to be coated in hot oil. Sauté for 5 minutes.
2. Add 2 teaspoons (10 ml) salt and 2 cups (500 ml) of water or vegetable broth. Simmer covered until all liquid is absorbed, about 15 to 20 minutes, stirring occasionally. Add 2 more cups (500 ml) of water, cover, and allow liquid to be fully absorbed. Taste rice to see if desired consistency is reached. If still too crunchy for you, add more water and continue cooking until satisfactory. Once cooked, remove from heat and set aside.
3. Add tahini, sesame seeds and nutritional yeast to rice and set aside.
4. In a large frying pan, heat 1 tablespoon (15 ml) of oil over medium heat and 1 clove of garlic. Add zucchini and stir. Add oregano and 1 teaspoon (5 ml) salt. Sauté over medium heat for about 15 minutes. Once cooked, add zucchini, including garlic and oil, to rice mixture. Set aside.
5. In a large frying pan, heat 1 tablespoon (15 ml) of oil over medium heat and 1 clove of garlic. Add in Cuban peppers. Add 1 teaspoon (5 ml) salt. Sauté over medium heat for about 5 minutes. Add mushrooms and cook an additional 5 minutes. Add Swiss chard and cook for about 3 to 4 minutes.
6. Once the vegetables are cooked, add them to the rice mixture.
7. Add chopped parsley to rice and stir. Heat rice over low heat until warm. Add black pepper and more salt, if desired, and sprinkle additional sesame seeds over dish for garnish. Serve warm.

*"You don't have a soul; you are a soul. You have a body." ~C.S. Lewis*

## Collard BLT Wraps with Tempeh Bacon

*As I have said many times now, vegans don't have to give up any of the flavors they love. Here's a crispy, tasty, and kind version of bacon, complete in a wrap BLT format!*

**Tempeh Bacon with marinade**

**Ingredients:**
*Makes approximately 4 to 6 servings*

½ package (120 g) tempeh, very thinly sliced
3 tablespoons (45 ml) grapeseed oil
1 teaspoon (5 ml) cumin
1 teaspoon (5 ml) paprika
2 teaspoons (10 ml) wheat-free tamari
2 teaspoons (10 ml) liquid smoke

¼ teaspoon (1.25 ml) cayenne pepper
½ teaspoon (2.5 ml) black pepper
1 clove of garlic, minced
Himalayan salt sprinkled over bacon once cooked, if desired

For frying pan: 4 tablespoons (60 ml) grapeseed oil
For baking: 2 tablespoons (30 ml) coconut oil or grapeseed oil or parchment paper

**Method:**
1. Slice the tempeh into very thin, rectangular slices.
2. To prepare the marinade, combine all other ingredients in a shallow dish and whisk until thoroughly mixed. If you'd like to make a larger amount of tempeh, double up on the marinade.
3. Brush marinade over tempeh strips evenly and allow tempeh to marinate for at least 15 minutes.
4. If you are frying, turn stovetop to medium-high heat, add grapeseed oil to the frying pan. Once oil has heated, lay the tempeh flat in the pan. Drizzle a bit of excess marinade onto the pan as the tempeh sizzles.
5. Allow to cook for 1 minute, then flip. Allow to cook for another minute on other side, or until both sides are crisp and browned.
6. If you are baking, preheat oven to 400°F (200°C). Spread coconut oil in glass casserole dish or baking sheet. Alternatively, you may line your casserole dish with parchment paper (no oil is required). Place tempeh single file. Bake for 15 minutes and flip over. Bake another 15 minutes or until strips are crispy. (Baked tempeh bacon will not be as crispy as when fried.)
7. Lay tempeh strips on paper towels to cool and to absorb excess oil. Sprinkle with Himalayan salt to taste.

## BLT Sauce

**Ingredients:**
⅓ cup (80 ml) vegan mayonnaise

2 tablespoons (30 ml) Dijon mustard
½ teaspoon (2.5 ml) chili flakes
1 tablespoon (15 ml) balsamic vinegar

1 tablespoon (15 ml) olive oil
1 tablespoon (15 ml) wheat-free tamari
1 clove of garlic, minced

**Method:**
1. Whisk all ingredients together in a small bowl.
2. Spread on collard leaves or whatever you are using for your wrap or bun.

## Collard Wraps

**Ingredients:**
4 to 6 large collard leaves, stems removed
2 cups (500 ml) alfalfa sprouts
4 large leaves of lettuce of your choice
2 tomatoes, sliced
½ cup (125 ml) green onion, thinly sliced

**Method:**
1. With a small, sharp knife, remove as much of the collard stem as possible. Lay leaf flat on a dish.
2. Brush 1 to 2 tablespoons (15 to 30 ml) of BLT sauce on the collard leaf.
3. Stack alfalfa sprouts, lettuce, tomato, green onion and 3 or 4 pieces of tempeh bacon (or more to taste).
4. Roll up the wrap and hold together with toothpicks.

## Amore's Chili Sin Carne

*Are you ready for a hug in a bowl? Talk about "comfort food"! This dish will warm your body and soul! You can customize the spiciness to your taste.*

**Ingredients:**
*Makes approximately 5 to 6 servings*
1 cup (250 ml) organic firm tofu
1 tablespoon (15 ml) olive oil
2 cloves of garlic, minced
1 teaspoon (5 ml) paprika
1 bay leaf
½ teaspoon (2.5 ml) cumin or chipotle
½ teaspoon (2.5 ml) red chili flakes
1 teaspoon (5 ml) oregano
¼ teaspoon (1.25 ml) cayenne pepper
2 tablespoons (30 ml) grapeseed oil
1 large white or red onion, chopped
1 tomato, chopped
1 teaspoon (5 ml) Himalayan salt, or more to taste
1 sweet potato, peeled and chopped
1 white potato, peeled and chopped
2 carrots, peeled and chopped
1 red bell pepper, seeds removed and chopped
½ cup (125 ml) tomato paste or strained tomatoes
1 cup (250 ml) kidney beans, cooked, or any beans of your choice (see tips in section "Soaking and Cooking Beans" on page 17)
1 cup (250 ml) organic frozen corn, cooked
1 cup (250 ml) spinach, chopped
½ teaspoon (2.5 ml) black pepper
½ cup (125 ml) fresh cilantro, chopped
Juice from ½ a lime (optional)

**Method:**
1. Slice your slab of tofu into thick pieces and pat dry with paper towels. You can leave the pieces of tofu on paper towels, with a compress on top, for 15 to 30 minutes to absorb excess moisture.
2. Crumble tofu with your hands into a large bowl. Add olive oil, garlic, paprika, bay leaf, cumin (or chipotle), chili, oregano and cayenne pepper. Mix well. Set aside and let marinate for a minimum of 20 to 30 minutes. If you have time to marinate for longer, cover the mixture and place it in the fridge.
3. Heat grapeseed oil on medium heat. Add onion, tomato and salt. Sauté for 2 to 3 minutes. Add potatoes and carrots and sauté for 5 minutes.
4. Remove bay leaf from marinated tofu and discard. Add tofu, red pepper and tomato paste to the pan with the vegetables and sauté for 10 minutes. Stir in cooked beans and corn. Continue to cook for 1 minute. Add spinach and stir. If all the vegetables are soft, turn off heat.
5. Taste test to see if you desire more salt or spices. Garnish with fresh cilantro and a splash of lime juice, if desired. Serve warm.

*"I have no doubt that it is a part of the destiny of the human race, in its gradual improvement, to leave off eating animals, as surely as the savage tribes have left off eating each other."*
*~Henry David Thoreau*

## Veggie Lover's Casserole

*With vegetable dishes this delicious, I am confident that I can make everyone love veggies! There are no rules for this one - add any and all vegetables you like. Try different versions and bliss out on health!*

**Ingredients:**
*Makes approximately 6 servings*

Mushroom Sauce (recipe follows)
4 potatoes, peeled and chopped
1 sweet potato, peeled and chopped
6 cloves of garlic, minced
2 tablespoons (30 ml) nutritional yeast
1 teaspoon (5 ml) dried chives
1 teaspoon (5 ml) onion powder
1 ½ (375 ml) cups of peas
3 tablespoons (45 ml) grapeseed oil
2 cups (500 ml) of broccoli, chopped
4 cups (1 L) Swiss chard, kale, spinach or rapini, stems removed and chopped
4 cups (1 L) of noodles of your choice (you can use gluten-free options)
1 tablespoon (15 ml) paprika
Himalayan salt
Thinly sliced jalapeño pepper, for garnish, if desired

**Ingredients for Mushroom Sauce:**
*Makes approximately 3 cups*

2 tablespoons (30 ml) grapeseed oil
2 cloves of garlic, minced
3 cups (750 ml) mushrooms, chopped
1 teaspoon (5 ml) Himalayan salt
1 teaspoon (5 ml) ground chipotle
½ cup (125 ml) raw cashews, soaked for 2 hours, drained
½ teaspoon (2.5 ml) oregano
2 tablespoons (30 ml) tahini
2 tablespoons (30 ml) olive oil
¼ cup (60 ml) nutritional yeast
¼ cup (60 ml) hemp seeds
½ teaspoon (2.5 ml) black pepper
1 ¼ (310 ml) cups water

**Method:**
1. To prepare the mushroom sauce, heat 2 tablespoons (30 ml) grapeseed oil in a large frying pan. Add 2 cloves of minced garlic. After 1 minute, add chopped mushrooms. Sprinkle salt and ground chipotle. Sauté until mushrooms are soft, about 3 to 5 minutes.
2. Place ⅔ of the mushrooms in a blender with the soaked cashews, oregano, tahini, olive oil, nutritional yeast, hemp seeds, black pepper and water. Blend until creamy.
3. Add remaining mushrooms to the sauce and set aside.
4. Place the chopped potatoes and sweet potato in a large pot and cover with water. Add one teaspoon (5 ml) of salt and 2 cloves of garlic. Bring to a boil, reduce heat to low and let simmer until potatoes are soft, about 15 to 20 minutes.
5. Once potatoes are cooked, drain water. Add 2 tablespoons (30 ml) nutritional yeast, chives, onion powder and 2 tablespoons (30 ml) of the mushroom sauce. Mash. Set aside.
6. Place peas in a small pot and cover with water. Bring to a boil and after 2 minutes, remove from heat and drain. Set aside.
7. In a large frying pan, heat 2 tablespoons (30 ml) grapeseed oil. Add 4 cloves of minced garlic and sauté for 2 minutes. Add chopped broccoli, sprinkle ½ teaspoon (2.5 ml) salt and sauté for 3 minutes, stirring frequently. Add chopped Swiss chard, spinach, kale or rapini. Sprinkle 1 teaspoon (5 ml) salt and sauté until wilted. Spinach will cook the fastest, whereas rapini or kale will take longer. Once cooked, remove from heat and set aside.
8. Cook your choice of pasta according to the instructions on the package. Drain.
9. In a large bowl, combine pasta and peas. Pour mushroom sauce over top and stir.
10. In a large glass casserole dish, place pasta and pea mixture as your bottom layer. Top it with the cooked broccoli and leafy greens. Spread the mashed potato mixture as the top and final layer. Sprinkle paprika for garnish and add thin slices of jalapeño pepper, if desired. Serve warm.

## Maria's Beany-Creamy Christmas Lasagna

*Lasagna is a typical main dish for any Italian Christmas lunch, and while usually scrumptious, not so commonly is it vegan. Necessity being the mother of invention, I created a vegan lasagna for Christmas day, or any day! You can easily render this dish gluten-free by opting for rice lasagna noodles.*

### Ingredients:
Makes approximately 10 servings
Basil Tomato Sauce (see recipe on page 76)
Vegan parmesan (see recipe on page 39).
Kidney Bean Cream (recipe follows)
3 tablespoons (45 ml) olive or grapeseed oil
2 cloves of garlic, chopped
4 cups (1 L) mushrooms (your favorite or a combination of different mushrooms), chopped
1 tablespoon (15 ml) unsalted steak spice (see page 69 for my homemade blend)
1 teaspoon (5 ml) fennel seeds
2 tablespoons (30 ml) oregano
5 cups (1 ¼ L) spinach, chopped, stems removed
1 large onion, chopped
4 small zucchini, chopped
2 cups (500 ml) fresh parsley, chopped
1 package eggless, whole-wheat or rice lasagna noodles (typically about 12 to 15 lasagna noodles)
Himalayan salt and black pepper to taste
For garnish: additional chopped parsley, chopped chili peppers if desired, and vegan parmesan

### Method:
1. Preheat oven to 350°F (180°C).
2. Prepare Basil Tomato Sauce (see recipe on page 76).
3. Prepare vegan parmesan (see recipe on page 39).
4. Prepare kidney bean cream (recipe follows).
5. Heat 1 tablespoon (15 ml) of oil in large frying pan over medium heat. Add garlic and sauté for 2 minutes.
6. Add mushrooms, one teaspoon (5 ml) each of salt, steak spice, fennel and 1 tablespoon (15 ml) of oregano and sauté until mushrooms are soft, about 4 or 5 minutes. Add spinach and ½ teaspoon (2.5 ml) of salt. Continue to sauté until spinach has completely wilted, about 1 to 2 minutes.
7. In a separate frying pan, heat 2 tablespoons (30 ml) of oil and add onions. Sauté for 2 to 3 minutes. Add zucchini, 1 tablespoon (15 ml) oregano and 1 teaspoon (5 ml) salt. Sauté until zucchini is soft, about 6 to 7 minutes. Add some of the chopped parsley.
8. Remove from heat and set veggies aside in a large bowl.
9. In a large pot, add water and salt and bring water to a boil. You can also use two pots of water and cook

half the package in each. The lasagna noodles benefit from a lot of water so that they do not break. Follow instructions on the box. Drain and set aside.
10. Spread one cup (250 ml) Basil Tomato sauce in large glass or ceramic baking dish.
11. Line lasagna noodles side by side to form bottom layer. Spread some veggies, kidney bean cream and vegan parmesan over the noodles. Add some tomato sauce to each layer. Repeat until last layer of lasagna is reached.
12. Over the last layer, spread remaining tomato sauce, vegan parmesan, chili flakes or chopped hot peppers (if desired) and garnish with fresh chopped parsley. Cover dish with aluminum foil. Perforate the foil in several places to allow the steam to escape as it bakes. Bake for 20 to 25 minutes. Remove from oven and serve warm.

*Kidney Bean Cream*

**Ingredients:**

2 cups (500 ml) kidney beans, cooked (see tips in section "Soaking and Cooking Beans" on page 17)
2 cloves of garlic, minced
1 ½ cups (375 ml) water
2 tablespoons (30 ml) olive oil
2 tablespoons (30 ml) fresh parsley, chopped
1 tablespoon (15 ml) nutritional yeast
1 tablespoon (15 ml) hemp seeds
1 ½ teaspoons (7.5 ml) salt

**Method:**
1. Blend all ingredients in a blender until smooth and creamy

*"Our mistreatment of animals is a spiritual problem. It reflects a misunderstanding that reduces beings to things." ~Dr. Will Tuttle*

## Moroccan Stuffed Zucchini

*Here comes another delicious recipe which makes use of the lovely, aromatic Ras el hanout spice blend. In addition to zucchini, you can also use this recipe to make stuffed peppers or stuffed eggplant. I used brown rice for its nutritional value, but you can use any rice you like, or quinoa.*

**Ingredients:**
Makes *approximately 6 servings*

4 tablespoons (60 ml) Ras el Hanout (see page 69 for recipe)
2 cups (500 ml) brown rice, cooked (or quinoa, cooked)
6 medium zucchini
1 small eggplant, skin removed and cubed
1 tablespoon (15 ml) olive oil
2 tablespoons (30 ml) grapeseed oil
1 small onion, diced
3 cloves garlic, minced
1 medium tomato, diced
1 cup (250 ml) chickpeas, cooked (see "Soaking and Cooking Beans" section on page 17 for tips)
3 tablespoons (45 ml) parsley, chopped
3 tablespoons (45 ml) pine nuts
Lemon zest from one lemon
Himalayan salt and ground black pepper to taste

**Method:**
1. Prepare Ras el Hanout (see recipe on page 69).
2. Cook rice (or quinoa) using any method suitable for the type of rice you have chosen and set aside.
3. Preheat oven to 400°F (200°C).
4. Chop off the tips of the zucchini. Chop each zucchini in half vertically. Chop halves in half horizontally. Two zucchini will produce 8 pieces. Remove seeds and interior of zucchini and chop into small pieces. Place in bowl.
5. Place zucchini on parchment-lined baking sheet and bake for about 15 minutes or until slightly soft. Set aside until cool.
6. Chop eggplant into small pieces and remove skin. Place in bowl with the pieces of the zucchini interior. Stir in 1 tablespoon (15 ml) each of olive oil and Ras el Hanout, making sure pieces of eggplant and zucchini are well coated.
7. Place eggplant and zucchini mixture on parchment-lined baking sheet and bake for 20 minutes.
8. In saucepan, heat 2 tablespoons (30 ml) grapeseed oil. Add onion and garlic. Sauté until soft. Stir in tomato and 1 tablespoon (15 ml) Ras el Hanout. Cook until tomato is soft, about 5 minutes. Remove saucepan from heat and stir in eggplant/zucchini mixture, rice, chickpeas, remaining Ras el Hanout, parsley, pine nuts, lemon zest, salt and pepper.
9. Stuff zucchini. Arrange on parchment-lined baking dish. Bake for 20 minutes. Serve warm.

# Portobello Burger

*This simple yet scrumptious burger is enhanced with a sauce of your choice. To top this heavenly burger, maybe you'd like to try the standard mustard and vegan mayo, my guacamole (page 55), or how about my heavenly hummus (page 42) or even the BLT sauce (page 82). Try them all and see which one you like best!*

**Ingredients:**
*Makes 2 burgers*

2 tablespoons (30 ml) grapeseed oil
2 large Portobello mushroom heads, stalks removed
4 teaspoons (20 ml) wheat-free tamari
Burger buns of your choice
Sauce of your choice
Raw veggies, lettuce and sprouts of your choice

**Method:**
1. Heat oil in pan on medium heat. Add mushrooms.
2. Add one teaspoon (5 ml) of tamari to each of the mushrooms and sauté for 2 to 3 minutes. Flip mushrooms over and add another teaspoon of tamari to each of the mushrooms and cook for another 2 to 3 minutes on that side.
3. Turn heat off, add mushroom to your burger bun and dress it up as your heart desires!

*"Don't ask what the world needs. Ask what makes you come alive, and go do it. Because what the world needs is people who have come alive." ~Howard Thurman*

## Sweet Potato Fries

*If you don't mind the slightly softer and sweeter version of fries, sweet potato is a nutritious alternative to regular potatoes. You can vary the spices to create any taste you like, depending on your culinary mood! You can also apply this method and recipe to white potatoes.*

### Ingredients:
Makes approximately 4 servings

2 large sweet potatoes, washed, cut into large wedges, with skins
3 tablespoons (45 ml) grapeseed oil
½ teaspoon (2.5 ml) paprika
½ teaspoon (2.5 ml) cumin
½ teaspoon (2.5 ml) black pepper
2 cloves of garlic, minced
½ teaspoon (2.5 ml) Himalayan salt

### Method:
1. Place potatoes in a large bowl and cover with cold water. Let stand for 20 minutes.
2. Preheat oven to 425°F (210°C).
3. Place parchment paper on cooking sheet to avoid having the potatoes stick.
4. Drain potatoes. Place the potato wedges on paper towels and pat dry.
5. Transfer potatoes to a clean, dry bowl and add oil, spices, garlic and salt. Toss to combine.
6. Arrange potato wedges in a single layer on the parchment paper.
7. Bake for 20 to 25 minutes. Gently turn potatoes after 10 minutes and return to the oven to finish baking.
8. Serve warm immediately once out of the oven.

## Bunless Tempeh Burger

*I have another burger idea for you, this one with tempeh. This is a bun-less version, but add a bun if you prefer!*

### Ingredients:
*Makes approximately 8 small burger patties*

1 package (240 g) tempeh, sliced into thin squares
2 tablespoons (30 ml) grapeseed oil
½ package sprouts of your choice (or sprout your own from seeds)
2 tomatoes, sliced
Mustard, vegan mayo (or whatever else you like on your burgers)

*Marinade for the tempeh*:

2 cloves of garlic, minced
3 tablespoons (45 ml) olive or grapeseed oil
1 tablespoon (15 ml) fennel seeds
3 tablespoons (45 ml) unsalted steak spice (see page 69 for my homemade blend)
1 teaspoon (5 ml) oregano

½ cup (125 ml) fresh parsley, chopped
½ teaspoon (2.5 ml) ground black pepper
2 tablespoons (30 ml) balsamic vinegar
2 tablespoons (30 ml) wheat-free tamari
1 bay leaf

### Method:
1. Marinate tempeh squares in marinade overnight (in the refrigerator) or for several hours.
2. In a large frying pan, heat grapeseed oil on medium heat. Sauté tempeh for about 3 to 4 minutes on each side, until slightly golden.
3. Add toppings to tempeh, slice of tomato and sprouts. Serve.

*"As long as men massacre animals, they will kill each other. Indeed, he who sows the seeds of murder and pain cannot reap the joy of love." ~Pythagoras*

## The Pasqualina: Kalamata Olive Pesto with Sautéed Kale and Sundried Tomatoes

*One of my favorite creations for sure, this dish is pure ecstasy for the taste buds. I was looking at my mother when I had a vision of this recipe, so naturally - I named it after her. It's as delicious as she is beautiful. As an alternative to this recipe, the kale can be added raw to the pasta.*

### Ingredients:
Makes approximately 4 to 5 servings

**Kalamata Pesto:**
2 cups (500 ml) kalamata olives, rinsed, pitted and chopped
1 clove of garlic, minced
1 teaspoon (5 ml) olive oil
1 teaspoon (5 ml) chili flakes
¼ cup (60 ml) fresh parsley, chopped
¼ cup (60 ml) nutritional yeast

**Pasta with Sautéed Kale and Sundried Tomatoes:**
3 tablespoons (45 ml) grapeseed oil
2 cloves of garlic, minced
4 cups (1 L) kale, stems removed and chopped
½ teaspoon (2.5 ml) Himalayan salt
½ cup (125 ml) unsalted, sulfite-free sundried tomatoes, chopped, pre-soaked for 1 hour
Pasta of your choice

### Method:
1. To make the kalamata olive pesto, blend the olives, garlic, olive oil, chili flakes, parsley and nutritional yeast in a food processor or blender until smooth and creamy. Set aside
2. In a large pot, heat grapeseed oil and minced garlic for about 2 minutes on medium heat.
3. Add chopped kale and salt and sauté for 4 to 5 minutes, stirring frequently.
4. Mix in sundried tomatoes and turn off heat.
5. Cook pasta according to instructions on the box and drain.
6. Add pasta to the pot with kale and sundried tomatoes. Stir. Place into serving plates or bowls. Scoop up desired amount of olive pesto and place on top of the pasta. Serve immediately.

### Lentil No-Meatloaf

*Be prepared for a taste explosion with this recipe! Not only is it totally flavorful, but it is also packed with so much nutrition. It makes the perfect family meal. This dish is particularly scrumptious with a side of creamy coleslaw (see recipe on page 49).*

**Ingredients:**
*Makes approximately 4 to 5 servings*

5 tablespoons (75 ml) ground flaxseed
½ cup (125 ml) water
3 tablespoons (45 ml) grapeseed oil
4 cloves of garlic, minced
1 red onion, finely chopped
2 carrots, peeled and shredded, and extra grated carrot for topping
1 small red bell pepper, finely chopped
1 celery stalk, finely chopped
½ cup (125 ml) fresh parsley, chopped
2 teaspoons (10 ml) oregano
1 teaspoon (5 ml) paprika
1 teaspoon (5 ml) fennel seeds
½ teaspoon (2.5 ml) cumin

½ teaspoon (2.5 ml) red chili flakes
½ teaspoon (2.5 ml) dried basil
1 cup (250 ml) French lentils, cooked
1 cup (250 ml) kidney beans, soaked overnight and cooked (see section on "Soaking and Cooking Beans" on page 17)
¼ cup (60 ml) raw pumpkin seeds
¼ cup (60 ml) raw sunflower seeds
½ cup (125 ml) chickpea flour
1 tablespoon (15 ml) Dijon mustard
2 teaspoons (10 ml) wheat-free tamari
Himalayan salt and black pepper
Small chunk of ginger, grated

**Method:**
1. Preheat oven to 350°F (180°C).
2. In a small bowl, combine flaxseed and water. Stir and set aside for 20 minutes.
3. Heat 2 tablespoons (30 ml) of oil in a frying pan, and add garlic, onion and a pinch of salt. Sauté for 4 to 5 minutes on low to medium heat.
4. Add another tablespoon (15 ml) of oil to the frying pan and add shredded carrots, pepper, and celery, with another pinch of salt. Sauté for 5 minutes.
5. Turn off heat. Add chopped parsley and spices. Stir in lentils and kidney beans.
6. Stir in seeds, chickpea flour and flaxseed. Add Dijon, tamari, black pepper and 2 teaspoons (10 ml) of salt. Let cool briefly.
7. Place mixture into food processor and blend briefly. Mixture should be chunky.
8. Taste test to see if you prefer more salt or spices.
9. Place parchment paper into rectangular casserole dish and pat down mixture.
10. Sprinkle grated ginger, carrot and a few sunflower and pumpkin seeds over top.
11. Bake for 50 minutes. Remove from oven and allow several minutes to cool before slicing.

*"It is not easy to find happiness in ourselves, and it is not possible to find it elsewhere."*
*~Agnus Repplier*

## Spring-Tasting Spring Rolls

With rice paper and rice noodles, this savory meal is naturally gluten-free. Rolling these takes a bit of practice, but the effort's worth it for something this yummy! I use **The Josephine** or my **Almond Arugula Pesto** as the sauce for my special Spring-inspired spring rolls. Try them both and see which one you prefer!

**Choice of Sauce:**
**The Josephine** (see page 46 for recipe. You will have to triple the recipe to have enough sauce for the rolls) or the **Almond Arugula Pesto** (see page 35 for recipe).

**Ingredients:**
*Makes approximately 15 rolls*

- 1 package rice or buckwheat Asian noodles
- 2 tablespoons (30 ml) sesame seeds
- 2 tablespoons (30 ml) black sesame seeds
- 4 carrots, peeled and sliced into long, thin strips
- 3 celery stalks, sliced into long, thin strips
- 1 red bell pepper, sliced into long, thin strips
- 1 daikon, peeled and sliced into long, thin strips

1 package rice paper
2 cups (500 ml) fresh parsley, cilantro or basil
4 cups (1 L) sprouts
2 cups (500 ml) arugula
Himalayan salt

**Method:**
1. Prepare your desired sauce.
2. Cook noodles according to package instructions. Drain and pour about half the amount of sauce onto noodles and stir. Sprinkle sesame seeds over noodles and set aside, covered, to cool.
3. Once all the vegetables have been sliced, and the noodles have cooled, you are ready to start preparing the spring rolls. You will need to use a work surface that does not stick too much to the rice paper. A glass surface is a better option than wood. You may also want to place a moist paper towel or clean, moist dishcloth on the surface and assemble the rolls on that.
4. Prepare a large bowl of warm water and dip a sheet of rice paper very briefly in the bowl. Lay the rice paper on your work surface.
5. Lay fresh parsley, cilantro or basil as your first layer in the center of the rice paper. (Once you form the rolls, the parsley or basil leaves will show through the thin rice paper.) Next, place a handful of noodles on the rice paper, leaving a space about 2 fingers in width at the top and bottom of the roll.
6. Add the sprouts and a few slices each of the carrot, daikon, celery and pepper.
7. Add about a teaspoon (or more to taste) of sauce over the vegetables. Add a few leaves of arugula.
8. Roll the rice paper by lifting the left side of the rice paper and bringing it over the vegetables. Next, bring the top part over, then the right side over to the left as tightly as you can. Be careful not to pierce the paper with any of the vegetables. Lastly, bring the bottom part over. Turn roll over until you see the parsley or basil. Your roll is complete. Place it on a serving dish. Serve immediately. If you wish to store your rolls, cover them with a moist paper towel and refrigerate them in an airtight container.

## Mung Bean Quinoa Pilaf

*This is such a fresh dish. The combination of dill and lemon makes it light, yet the quinoa and mung beans make it very nutrient-rich and filling. This dish is perfect for a summer meal.*

### Ingredients:
*Makes approximately 4 servings*

½ cup (125 ml) mung beans, soaked overnight
¼ cup (60 ml) red quinoa
¾ cup (180 ml) white quinoa
2 tablespoons (30 ml) grapeseed oil
1 cup (250 ml) green onions, chopped
2 cups (500 ml) mushrooms, chopped
2 cups (500 ml) vegetable broth (see recipe on page 30) or 2 cups water
¾ cup (180 ml) green peas, cooked
⅓ cup (80 ml) lemon juice, freshly squeezed
2 tablespoons (30 ml) lemon zest
3 tablespoons (45 ml) fresh dill, chopped
Himalayan salt and freshly ground black pepper to taste

### Method:
1. To cook the pre-soaked mung beans, in a small pot, add 3 cups of water with the mung beans and bring to a boil. Reduce heat and simmer, covered, for about 10 to 15 minutes. Once beans are very soft, drain excess water. Set aside.
2. In a sauce pan over medium heat, toast quinoa for about 5 minutes, stirring occasionally. Set aside in a bowl.
3. In the same saucepan, heat oil and add onions with a pinch of salt. Sauté until soft. Add mushrooms and sauté until slightly soft, about 4 or 5 minutes.
4. Add quinoa and vegetable broth. Bring to a boil and then reduce heat to simmer. Cook covered until all the liquid has absorbed, about 15 minutes.
5. Once quinoa is cooked, add mung beans, peas, lemon juice, lemon zest, dill and salt and pepper to taste. Garnish with a sprig of dill. Serve warm.

*"Humanity's true moral test, its fundamental test consists of its attitude towards those who are at its mercy: animals. And in this respect humankind has suffered a fundamental debacle, a debacle so fundamental that all others stem from it." ~Milan Kundera*

## Splendid Spelt Gnocchi

*My favorite type of pasta has always been gnocchi! Pillowy soft, light and vegan is the way I like my gnocchi! It's a little challenging to form the gnocchi, but remember, practice makes perfect! The spelt flour is a gluten-friendly option, however unbleached white flour is the most common flour used in making gnocchi. It's important to use starchy potatoes like Russet potatoes to create the light texture that we're looking for.*

**Ingredients:**
Makes approximately 6 to 8 servings

5 Russet potatoes
6 cups (1 ½ L) spelt flour
Himalayan salt
Water

**Method:**
1. Peel and chop potatoes into large chunks. Place them in a large pot and cover with water. Add one teaspoon of salt. Bring to a boil. (Alternatively, potatoes may be boiled whole, with the skins on. Once they have cooled slightly, the skins can be easily removed with your fingers.)

2. Boil for approximately 20 minutes or until potatoes are soft. Before draining, pour 1 cup (250 ml) of the potato water into a bowl or cup and set aside. Drain the rest of the water.
3. While the potatoes are still warm, add about ¼ cup (60 ml) of the potato water to the potatoes and mash.
4. On your work surface, place 4 cups (1 L) of flour in a tire-like shape and form a well in the center. Keep the rest of the flour on the side. Place your mashed potatoes in the well. Sprinkle small amount of salt over flour and potatoes, approximately 1 teaspoon (5 ml).
5. With your hands, work the flour into the potatoes. Form a well in the center and add ¼ cup (60 ml) of the potato water.
6. Start kneading the mixture. Flour should start sticking together. Make another well and add another ¼ cup (60 ml) of water.
7. You should now be able to make a log-shaped mound of soft dough. Sprinkle flour over mound so it does not stick to your fingers. Always sprinkle your work surface with flour as well.
8. Cut off a small piece of dough and flatten it out with your hands. Cut long rope-like strips, about one inch thick, and roll them out a little over the flour on the work surface.
9. Cut rope into square-shaped pieces about the size of a thumb nail. Always sprinkle a small amount of flour over the pieces so they don't stick.
10. To form the shape of the gnocchi, take the square piece and press down gently with your index and middle fingers on your work surface. Alternatively, you can press the gnocchi down with your fingers off the back of a fork or use a ridged gnocchi paddle. This will create ridged-shaped gnocchi.
11. Once all your gnocchi are formed, you can drop them into your salted boiling water if you want to cook them right away. Boil them for about 5 minutes. Gnocchi will float when cooked.
12. If you wish to freeze them, lay them flat, in a single file, on a baking sheet lined with parchment paper. Once they are frozen, you can transfer them to a freezer bag. When you wish to cook them, drop them frozen into salted boiling water.
13. Serve them with any sauce of your choice. I like them best with my Basil Tomato Sauce (see recipe on page 76).

## Pizza Vegana

*You're the boss when it comes to what toppings you want on your pizza. Aside from a plethora of delicious veggies and spices, there is a large variety of vegan cheeses, pepperoni and sausages you can try. To make an Italian **"white pizza"** (no tomatoes), try garlic powder, oregano, olive oil, rosemary, Himalayan salt and black pepper.*

### Ingredients:
Makes 2 small (11-inch, 28 cm) pizzas

1 package dry active yeast
¼ cup (60 ml) warm water
1 teaspoon (5 ml) raw cane sugar
1 cup (250 ml) water
¼ cup (60 ml) olive oil
1 teaspoon (5 ml) Himalayan salt
3 cups (750 ml) unbleached white flour or spelt flour

Pizza toppings of your choice, such as seen above, sliced mushrooms, onions, strained tomatoes, oregano, sliced onions, vegan cheese, and chipotle.

### Method:
1. To prepare the yeast, mix the dry yeast into a glass with ¼ cup (60 ml) of warm water. Mix in the sugar. Set aside for about 15 minutes.
2. To prepare the dough, I use a very large pot. Add the water, oil and salt. When the yeast is ready, add to the pot and stir gently.
3. Slowly add in the flour and mix with a fork or your fingers. As dough begins to form, knead it for about 5 minutes and make a mound. Pat a small amount of olive oil on the surface of the mound to keep it moist.
4. Cover the pot with a clean dish cloth and set aside for at least one hour to let the dough rise.
5. Once the dough has risen, preheat your oven to 350°F.
6. Take ½ of the dough and flatten it out with your hands. If you are feeling adventurous, you can make use of your knuckles and throw the pizza dough in the air! It is important to flatten and stretch out the dough as evenly as possible. If you make a tear in the dough, you can patch it up, or bunch up the dough and start over.
7. Mold the stretched out dough in a circular or square shape on your baking sheet. Place in the oven and bake for 10 minutes. Remove from the oven and top the pizza as you desire.
8. Place back in the oven for another 10 to 15 minutes, or until the pizza is cooked.

**"We must not refuse to see with our eyes what they must endure with their bodies." ~Gretchen Wyler**

# Curried Chickpeas with Couscous

*Curry is a very tasty and aromatic spice blend which can give an Indian flare to any dish. You can make your own curry, or buy the blend already prepared. I used the Madras curry blend here, but you can use any curry you like best.*

### Ingredients:
*Makes approximately 4-6 servings*

8 Roman tomatoes
2 cups (500 ml) whole wheat or spelt couscous
2 cups (500 ml) water
2 tablespoons (30 ml) olive oil
3 teaspoons (15 ml) oregano
1 ¼ cup (310 ml) fresh parsley, chopped
2 tablespoons (30 ml) grapeseed oil
2 white onions, chopped
4 cloves of garlic, minced
1 teaspoon (5 ml) dried basil
1 teaspoon (5 ml) chili flakes
2 cups (500 ml) chickpeas, cooked (see section "Soaking and Cooking Beans" on page 17 for tips)
2 tablespoons (30 ml) Madras curry
1 tablespoon (15 ml) fresh ginger, minced
Himalayan salt and black pepper to taste

### Method:
1. Bring a pot of water to a boil. Drop tomatoes into the boiling water for 1 to 2 minutes.
2. Remove pot from the stove and drain. Let tomatoes cool before peeling and dicing them.
3. Once tomatoes are cooled, peel the skins off with your fingers and discard. Chop interior of tomatoes and place in a small bowl. Set aside.
4. To prepare the couscous, pour 2 cups (500 ml) of water into a pot and bring to a boil. Remove from heat and stir in couscous. Let sit, covered, until all water is absorbed and couscous is light and fluffy.
5. To the couscous, add olive oil, 2 teaspoons (10 ml) oregano, 2 teaspoons (10 ml) salt and ¼ cup (60 ml) of chopped parsley. Set aside.
6. In a large pan, heat grapeseed oil on medium heat. Add chopped onions and garlic. Sauté until onions are soft and garlic is slightly golden, about 5 minutes.
7. Add chopped tomatoes, 2 teaspoons (10 ml) salt, 1 teaspoon (5 ml) oregano, basil and chili flakes. Lower heat. Let simmer for 5 minutes.
8. Add cooked chickpeas, 1 teaspoon (5 ml) salt, curry, ginger and remaining parsley. Let simmer for 5 minutes. Turn off heat. Add black pepper if desired. Serve warm over couscous.

## Carnaval Tacos Veganos with Mexican Bean and Corn Salad

Like I always say: if vegan is this delicious, why not vegan? My secret is: the choice of spices, which I share with you below. I named this dish after one of my all-time favorite pick-me-up songs by the legendary **Celia Cruz, "La Vida es un Carnaval"**. For those of you looking for an alternative to tofu, you may use cannellini, black or kidney beans. Try these tacos with my delicious **Mexican Bean and Corn Salad** (recipe follows). Don't forget to play the tune while making this dish!

**Ingredients:**
Makes approximately 6 tacos
1 package (454 g) organic firm tofu
5 tablespoons (75 ml) grapeseed oil
½ teaspoon (2.5 ml) ground chipotle
1 teaspoon (5 ml) paprika
½ teaspoon (2.5 ml) cumin
1 teaspoon (5 ml) oregano
1 package soft tortillas of your choice
½ teaspoon (2.5 ml) chili flakes
½ teaspoon (2.5 ml) black pepper
2 cloves of garlic, minced
1 tablespoon (15 ml) balsamic vinegar
1 tablespoon (15 ml) wheat-free tamari
1 onion, chopped
½ red bell pepper, chopped
1 teaspoon (5 ml) Himalayan salt

Topping for tacos, as desired: shredded lettuce or cabbage, tomatoes, hot peppers, vegan shredded cheese

**Method:**
1. Slice tofu into thick slabs and lay on paper towels to allow excess moisture to be absorbed. Cover with paper towels. You can apply a weight on top of the paper towels, such as another dish. Let stand for about 15 to 20 minutes.
2. Crumble tofu into a large bowl. Add all ingredients for marinade: 3 tablespoons (45 ml) grapeseed oil, chipotle, paprika, cumin, oregano, chili flakes, pepper, minced garlic, balsamic vinegar and tamari. Allow to marinate for about an hour.
3. Heat 2 tablespoons (30 ml) of grapeseed oil in a large frying pan. Add chopped onion, red pepper, sprinkle salt, and sauté until soft, about 5 minutes.
4. Add marinated tofu and sauté for about 7 to 8 minutes. The tofu may start to stick to the frying pan, so be sure to scrape it into the mixture. The browned tofu gives it extra flavor.
5. Once the tofu is cooked, remove from heat, cover and set aside.

6. In another frying pan, heat a very small amount of grapeseed oil and drop your soft tortilla into it. Allow the tortilla to brown slightly, about 1 to 2 minutes, and then flip over.
7. Place warm tortilla in a serving dish and add tofu. Top the taco as you like, with shredded iceberg lettuce or cabbage, diced tomatoes, hot peppers and vegan cheese.

## Mexican Bean and Corn Salad

**Ingredients:**
*Makes approximately 6 servings*

3 cups (750 ml) organic corn, cooked
2 cups (500 ml) black or kidney beans, cooked
(see tips in section "Soaking and Cooking Beans" on page 17)
4 green onions, chopped
¼ red bell pepper, chopped
1 red chili pepper, chopped (optional)
1 small tomato, chopped
1 avocado, chopped (optional)
1 tablespoon (15 ml) olive oil
1 clove of garlic, minced
1 teaspoon (5 ml) oregano
1 cup (250 ml) fresh cilantro, chopped
Juice from one lime
Himalayan salt and black pepper to taste

**Method:**
1. Combine all ingredients in a large bowl and toss. You may serve it immediately, or chill it in the refrigerator before serving.

*"'Thou shalt not kill' does not apply to murder of one's own kind only, but to all living beings; this Commandment was inscribed in the human breast long before it was proclaimed from Sinai."*
*~Leo Tolstoy*

## Pasta e Fagioli with Homemade Tagliatelle

*Pasta and beans? Oh yes, this dish is truly an Italian classic! Any type of small pasta works here – you don't require homemade pasta. However, if you're feeling adventurous, here is my homemade pasta recipe for "tagliatelle" which are like fettucini, but cut shorter. You require a pasta maker and rolling pin to make this pasta.*

### Pasta e Fagioli

**Ingredients:**
*Makes approximately 4 servings*

6 Roman tomatoes
2 tablespoons (30 ml) grapeseed oil
5 cloves of garlic, minced
1 celery stalk or celery heart
6 fresh basil leaves
2 teaspoons (10 ml) Himalayan salt (or more to taste)
⅓ cup (80 ml) fresh parsley, chopped
1 ½ cups (375 ml) pinto or kidney beans, cooked (see tips in section "Soaking and Cooking Beans" on page 17)
½ teaspoon (2.5 ml) black pepper (or more to taste)

6 cups (1 ½ L) of water
Small pasta of your choice or homemade spelt tagliatelle (recipe below)

**Method:**
1. Bring a pot of water to a boil. Drop tomatoes into the boiling water for 1 to 2 minutes.
2. Remove pot from the stove and drain. Let tomatoes cool before peeling and dicing them.
3. In a large pot, heat grapeseed oil on medium heat and add minced garlic. Brown garlic slightly, about 1 to 2 minutes.
4. Add diced tomatoes, celery, basil, and a teaspoon of salt. Let simmer for about 20 minutes.
5. Remove celery and basil leaves and discard. Add chopped parsley, cooked beans and black pepper.
6. Add 6 cups (1 ½ L) of water and bring to a boil. Add pasta. Reduce heat and simmer until pasta is cooked. Most of the water will be absorbed by the pasta, but some excess liquid is desired, as with a stew. Taste test to see if more salt or pepper is desired. You can sprinkle some vegan parmesan over top if desired (see recipe on page 39). Serve warm.

*Spelt Tagliatelle*

**Ingredients:**
3 cups (750 ml) spelt flour, extra flour on the side
Himalayan salt
¾ cup (180 ml) water

**Method:**
1. Pour flour onto work station in a well formation. Keep an extra amount of flour on the side for sprinkling over dough when it gets sticky.
2. Sprinkle small amount of salt over flour well (about ½ teaspoon, 2.5 ml).
3. Pour water slowly into well a bit at a time, working flour into the water gently with your fingers or a fork.
4. Once firm, knead dough for about 5 minutes. Sprinkle small amounts of flour onto work station and dough if it becomes too sticky.
5. Form a loaf and let loaf sit for 15 to 30 minutes.
6. Sprinkle small amount of flour over dough. With a rolling pin, flatten the dough. Cut small amounts and pass through the pasta maker at the setting which will further flatten the dough (No. 8 setting).
7. Lay pieces of flattened dough on flour-sprinkled work station to avoid sticking.
8. Pass all the pieces of dough, one by one, through the fettucini setting of the pasta maker. Lay pasta on flour-sprinkled work station. Once all the pasta is ready, bring your tomato and bean mixture to a boil. Add pasta and cook for about 7 minutes or until pasta is very soft.
9. If you would like to keep some pasta for another recipe, you can freeze the pasta. (Lay it flat, single layer, on a cooking sheet and once it is completely frozen, transfer it to a freezer bag.)

## Sweet Potato Veggie Bean Cotoletta with Iceberg Lemon Salad

*As you've noticed by now, I veganize everything, including breaded cutlets, known as "cotoletta" in Italian. For this dish, I combined a whole bunch of organic veggies and black beans, then breaded and baked them. You can also fry them, as is typical for cutlets, but I find it easier to bake. I also appreciate the fact that with a parchment paper covering the baking dish, we don't have to use any additional oil. I love these served with iceberg lettuce and a simple lemon vinaigrette (recipe below).*

**Ingredients:**
*Makes approximately 12 small cutlets*
5 tablespoons (75 ml) ground flaxseed
½ cup (125 ml) water
3 tablespoons (45 ml) grapeseed oil
1 cup (250 ml) kale, stems removed, chopped
1 cup (250 ml) broccoli florets, chopped
2 tomatoes, chopped
2 celery stalks, chopped
2 carrots, peeled and chopped
1 bell pepper, chopped
1 sweet potato, peeled and chopped
1 onion, chopped
6 cloves of garlic, minced
1 tablespoon (15 ml) fresh ginger, minced
1 tablespoon (15 ml) steak spice (see page 69 for my homemade blend)
1 teaspoon (5 ml) coriander
1 teaspoon (5 ml) cumin
1 teaspoon (5 ml) ground chipotle
2 teaspoons (10 ml) Himalayan salt, more to taste
1 cup (250 ml) fresh parsley, chopped
2 cups (500 ml) black beans, presoaked and cooked (see "Soaking and Cooking Beans" section on page 17)
¾ cup (180ml) bread crumbs (see page 73 for recipe)
1 cup (250 ml) kamut flour

**Method:**
1. Preheat oven to 400°F (200°C).
2. Line baking dish with parchment paper and set aside.
3. In a small bowl, combine flaxseed and water and set aside.
4. In a large pot, heat grapeseed oil on medium heat. Add all chopped veggies (veggies must be chopped into very small pieces), including onion, garlic and ginger. Add all spices and salt. Sauté on medium heat for about 15 minutes, or until all vegetables are very soft. Remove from heat.
5. Add chopped parsley and beans. Mash with a potato masher. Add soaked flaxseed, ½ cup (125 ml) bread crumbs and flour. Mix well. Set remaining bread crumbs aside to use for coating the cutlets.
6. Place half of the mixture into a food processor and blend briefly. Return mixture to pot with mashed veggies and mix well.
7. Form patties by taking a small amount of veggie mixture with your hands and coat with bread crumbs. Lay the patties on the parchment paper.
8. Place in the oven to bake, uncovered, for 30 minutes. Flip them over after 15 minutes.
9. Remove from oven. You can sprinkle more salt over top if desired.


*Iceberg Lemon Salad*

**Ingredients:**

1 head of iceberg lettuce, chopped
Juice from 1 or 2 lemons
2 tablespoons (30 ml) olive oil
Himalayan salt and black pepper to taste


**Method:**
1. In large salad bowl, combine lettuce, oil and juice from one lemon. Add salt and black pepper to taste. Toss. Taste test to see if salad has enough lemon for your liking. If desired, you can add the juice from a second lemon.


*"Life begets life. Energy creates energy. It is by spending oneself that one becomes rich."*
*~Sarah Bernhard*

## Maria's Summer Fiesta Pasta Salad

*It's hard to beat the tastiness of pasta! With so many ways to prepare it and a huge variety of tasty sauces, is there anything more versatile than pasta? Here's a cold pasta and vegetable dish that is lovely for summer picnics. Any type of pasta can work and gluten-free options are plentiful. In the picture above, you see organic wholegrain spelt spiral noodles.*

### Ingredients:
Makes approximately 6 servings

4 cups (1 L) small pasta noodles of your choice, cooked
8 green onions, chopped
2 carrots, chopped
2 celery stalks, chopped
1 cup (250 ml) hearts of palm, chopped
½ cup (125 ml) sulfite-free sundried tomatoes, chopped
⅓ cup (80 ml) fresh parsley, chopped

### Dressing:

½ cup (125 ml) vegan mayonnaise
¼ cup (60 ml) nutritional yeast
2 cloves of garlic, minced
Juice from ½ a lemon
3 tablespoons (45 ml) olive oil

1 teaspoon (5 ml) oregano
1 teaspoon (5 ml) black pepper
1 teaspoon (5 ml) mustard powder
½ teaspoon (2.5 ml) Himalayan salt

### Method:
1. Cook pasta as per instructions on the box. Drain and set aside to cool.
2. In a small bowl, combine all dressing ingredients and mix thoroughly.
3. In a large bowl, combine cooled pasta, onion, carrots, celery, hearts of palm, sundried tomatoes and parsley.
4. Pour dressing over pasta and vegetables and toss.
5. Place in the refrigerator for 20 to 30 minutes to chill and let flavors fully marinate. Garnish with more chopped fresh parsley, if desired. Serve chilled.

## Tandori Tempeh with Spiced Sweet Potato Mash

*This is an incredibly savory and spicy, Indian-inspired dish with nutrient-dense tempeh. Very easy and quick to prepare, it is so full of flavor that the whole family will love it! Serve it with my sweet potato mash and a salad.*

### Ingredients:
*Makes approximately 4 servings*

1 package (240 g) tempeh
2 tomatoes, diced
1 onion, chopped
3 red chili peppers, chopped

### Marinade:

¼ cup (60 ml) water
2 tablespoons (30 ml) grapeseed or olive oil
3 cloves of garlic, minced
1 ½ teaspoons (7.5 ml) paprika
1 teaspoon (5 ml) turmeric
½ teaspoon (2.5 ml) coriander
½ teaspoon (2.5 ml) cumin

½ teaspoon (2.5 ml) ginger
½ teaspoon (2.5 ml) cardamom
½ teaspoon (2.5 ml) black pepper
¼ teaspoon (1.25 ml) cayenne pepper
2 tablespoons (30 ml) wheat-free tamari
1 tablespoon (15 ml) Dijon mustard
2 tablespoons (30 ml) chia seeds

**Method:**
1. Preheat oven to 350°F (180°C).
2. Tempeh is usually frozen when purchased. Thaw out and slice into thin squares.
3. Prepare the marinade for the tempeh by mixing all the marinade ingredients in a bowl, except the chia seeds.
4. Line large baking dish with parchment paper to avoid sticking. Place tempeh squares, single layer, on the paper. Pour marinade and vegetables over tempeh. Sprinkle chia seeds over top.
5. Cover dish with aluminum foil. Perforate foil in a few places to allow steam to escape as it bakes.
6. Bake for 30 minutes total. After 15 minutes, remove from the oven, turn tempeh squares over, discard aluminum foil and return to the oven, uncovered, for the remaining 15 minutes.
7. Serve warm.


*Spiced Sweet Potato Mash*

**Ingredients:**

2 sweet potatoes, peeled and chopped
3 white potatoes, peeled and chopped
2 cloves of garlic, chopped
2 tablespoons (30 ml) nutritional yeast
2 tablespoons (30 ml) vegan butter
1 tablespoon (15 ml) turmeric
1 tablespoon (15 ml) paprika
Himalayan salt and black pepper to taste


**Method:**
1. Placed chopped potatoes in a large pot and cover with water. Add salt, about 1 teaspoon (5 ml), and chopped garlic. Bring to a boil. Lower heat and let simmer until potatoes are very soft, about 20 minutes.
2. Drain all water. Add nutritional yeast, vegan butter, turmeric, paprika and mash with a potato masher. Taste test to see if more salt is desired. Add black pepper to taste. Serve warm.


**"Enchant, stay beautiful and graceful, but do this, eat well. Bring the same consideration to the preparation of your food as you devote to your appearance. Let your dinner be a poem, like your dress."**
**~Charles Pierre Monselet**

# Desserts and Snacks

## Triple Chocolate Coconut Cupcakes

*Triple chocolate? This much vegan decadence is almost indecent! I combined the flavors of rich chocolate and creamy, nutty coconut to create the most delicious cupcakes ever!*

**Ingredients:**
*Makes 12 cupcakes*

**Chocolate Cupcakes:**
1 ½ cups (375 ml) unbleached white flour
⅓ cup (80 ml) cacao powder
½ teaspoon (2.5 ml) baking soda
½ teaspoon (2.5 ml) Himalayan salt
2 teaspoons (10 ml) unsweetened coconut flakes
2 teaspoons (10 ml) non-dairy chocolate chips
1 cup (250 ml) raw cane sugar
½ cup (125 ml) grapeseed oil

1 cup (250 ml) coconut water
2 teaspoons (10 ml) vanilla extract
2 tablespoons (30 ml) apple cider vinegar

**Chocolate Frosting:**

1 ¾ cups (430 ml) icing sugar
¼ cup (60 ml) cacao powder
1 cup (250 ml) vegan butter
1 teaspoon (5 ml) vanilla extract
1 to 2 teaspoons (5 to 10 ml) water

**Topping over frosting:**

Unsweetened coconut flakes
Non-dairy chocolate chips

**Method:**
1. Preheat oven to 350°F (180°C). Line cupcake pan with parchment cups.
2. In a large bowl, mix flour, cacao, baking soda, salt, coconut flakes, chocolate chips and sugar. In another bowl, combine oil, coconut water and vanilla. Pour liquid ingredients into dry ingredients, and mix until smooth.
3. Add vinegar and stir briefly. Quickly spoon batter into cupcake pan.
4. Bake for 20 minutes, or until toothpick test comes out dry. Allow muffins to cool completely before adding frosting. It's best to refrigerate them for a couple of hours and then add frosting later.
5. To prepare the frosting, combine all frosting ingredients in a large bowl, starting with only one teaspoon of water. With a handheld cake mixer, whip until smooth and creamy, but firm. If mixture is too powdery, add extra teaspoon of water.
6. Add frosting to cupcakes once they have fully cooled using cake decorating kit. Top frosting with coconut flakes and chocolate chips.

*"Cooking demands attention, patience, and above all, respect for the gifts of the earth. It is a form of worship, a way of giving thanks." ~Judith B. Jones*

## Classic Italian Taralli

*An old Italian recipe made even better now that it's veganized! Taralli are a classic snack in any Italian household. They are sometimes considered the Italian version of breadsticks. I don't know if it's the pepper or the fennel seeds, but something is clearly addictive about these little treats! They can be served to accompany soups, but mostly Italians love them as a snack with a glass of wine.*

**Ingredients:**
*Makes approximately 40 taralli*

¼ cup (60 ml) warm water
1 teaspoon (5 ml) cane sugar
1 package of active dry yeast
1 cup (250 ml) water
½ cup (125 ml) olive oil
1 ½ teaspoons (7.5 ml) Himalayan salt
1 teaspoon (5 ml) black pepper
1 teaspoon (5 ml) fennel seeds
3 cups (750 ml) unbleached white flour

**Method:**
1. To prepare the yeast, pour ¼ cup (60 ml) of warm water into a glass. Add the sugar and stir. Add the package of yeast and stir gently. Set aside for 10 minutes to activate the yeast. It should approximately double in size.
2. Into a large pot, pour in water and olive oil. Stir in salt, pepper and fennel seeds.
3. Once the yeast is ready after about 10 minutes, stir into liquid mixture.
4. Add flour to liquid mixture slowly, about ½ cup (125 ml) at a time and begin kneading the dough in the pot. It will be very sticky. You can coat your hands with some olive oil to prevent the dough from sticking to your hands too much.
5. Once you have finished adding all the flour, make a mound of dough in the pot and lightly coat the top with a small amount of olive oil. Cover the pot with a clean, dry dishcloth. Set aside and allow the dough to rise for about 1 hour.
6. Brush some olive oil on your work station. Pull off a small chunk of dough and begin rolling the dough into a thin rope. Shape the taralli into a circle or into a long braid. Make sure the dough is thin because it will continue to rise as it bakes. Lay the taralli onto cooking sheets.
7. Preheat your oven to 350°F (180°C). Once all your taralli are formed, place them into the oven and bake them for 35 to 50 minutes. Start checking them after 30 minutes. Once they are slightly golden, they are done.
8. Remove from the oven and lay them flat onto a clean tablecloth to cool. They will get crispy as they cool.
9. Serve once they are thoroughly cooled, as you would breadsticks.

## Anna's Blueberry Cake

*My cousin, Anna, and I used to love this blueberry cake that our mothers made when we were little. I decided to veganize that old family recipe (previously never written down) and name it after her!*

**Ingredients:**

**Cake:**
4 cups (1 L) unbleached white flour
1 cup (250 ml) raw cane sugar
4 teaspoons (20 ml) baking powder
4 teaspoons (20 ml) egg replacer
½ teaspoon (2.5 ml) Himalayan salt
1 cup (250 ml) grapeseed oil
1 cup (250 ml) water

**Fruit Filling:**
Your favorite pie filling. Anna's favorite is blueberry.
Or
3 cups (750 ml) fresh or frozen berries (thawed and drained) of your choice, save a few berries on the side. Blend fruits in a blender with ⅓ cup (80 ml) raw agave nectar. Add in the remaining whole or chopped berries.

**Topping:**
⅓ cup (80 ml) almond flour
⅓ cup (80 ml) raw cane sugar
3 teaspoons (15 ml) vegan butter

**Method:**

1. Preheat oven to 350°F (180°C).
2. Combine cake ingredients in a large bowl.
3. Knead mixture into firm loaf. Remove ⅓ of the mixture and set aside.
4. Press down remaining mixture in a square glass or ceramic baking dish.
5. Pour in fruit filling.
6. With remaining cake mixture, take small amounts and make palm-sized patches with your hands. Place patch by patch over fruit filling until all the fruit is completely covered.
7. In a small bowl, combine all topping ingredients. Rub mixture between fingers until it begins to form small clumps. Sprinkle crumble topping over top.
8. Bake for 50 minutes. Remove from oven and allow to cool for at least 1 ½ to 2 hours before slicing.
9. Serve with fresh berries, if desired.

*"Wisdom is knowing I am nothing; Love is knowing I am everything,
and between the two my life moves."
~Sri Nisargadatta Maharaj*

## Orange Sunrise Bran Muffins with Creamy Dreamy Almond Milk

*Delightfully orangey and light tasting, this muffin is equally delicious with dates or raisins.*

**Ingredients:**
*Makes approximately 12 large muffins*

Dry ingredients:
1 ½ cups (375 ml) bran
1 ½ cups (375 ml) whole wheat pastry flour or spelt flour
4 teaspoons (20 ml) egg replacer
2 teaspoons (10 ml) baking powder
1 teaspoon (5 ml) baking soda
⅓ cup (80 ml) raisins (or fresh dates, pitted and chopped)
1 teaspoon (5 ml) pumpkin pie spice
¼ teaspoon (1.25 ml) Himalayan salt

Wet ingredients:
1 cup (250 ml) plain unsweetened almond milk (store-bought or see below for my Creamy Dreamy Almond Milk recipe)
½ cup (125 ml) grapeseed oil
½ cup (125 ml) raw agave nectar
Juice and zest from one orange

**Method:**
1. Preheat oven to 350°F (180°C).
2. In a large bowl, mix all dry ingredients, including raisins or chopped dates.
3. In a separate bowl, mix all wet ingredients, including orange zest.
4. Pour wet ingredients into dry ingredients and stir with a spatula.
5. Line muffin pan with parchment baking cups.
6. Spoon mixture into cups.
7. Bake for 18 to 20 minutes, or until toothpick test comes out dry.

## Creamy Dreamy Almond Milk

**Ingredients:**
*Makes approximately 5 cups of milk*

2 cups (500 ml) almonds, soaked overnight and drained
5 cups (1 ¼ L) water
4 dates, pitted (optional)
1 teaspoon (5 ml) vanilla extract (optional)

**Method:**

1. Combine almonds and water in a high-powered blender and blend until liquefied.
2. Add pitted dates and/or vanilla extract if desired. Blend.
3. Pour liquid through cheese cloth or nut milk bag and squeeze into a large bowl.
4. Store nut milk in a glass jar. The milk may be refrigerated for up to 4 days. The almond pulp can be frozen for later use in other recipes. To make a thicker, creamier milk, use less water.

## Cacao Goddess Pudding

*One of the comments I received about this pudding is that it is multilayered, with perfectly balanced flavors. Every spoonful gives you a hint of the various ingredients combined to perfection. Creamy, rich and sweet, this pudding will quickly become a favorite!*

### Ingredients:
*Makes approximately 6 servings*

1 cup (250 ml) organic soft tofu
1 large ripe banana
1 cup (250 ml) raw cacao powder
1 teaspoon (5 ml) vanilla extract
½ cup (125 ml) raw agave nectar

2 teaspoons (10 ml) cashew butter
¼ cup (60 ml) unsweetened almond milk (see page 120 for homemade recipe)
1 tablespoon (15 ml) chicory coffee substitute
Fresh mint leaves and berries of your choice for garnish

### Method:
1. Combine all ingredients in a blender or food processor. Blend until soft and creamy.
2. Refrigerate for 2 hours so that pudding becomes firm. Serve with a garnish of fresh mint leaves and berries of your choice, if desired.

*"You can succeed at almost anything for which you have unbridled enthusiasm." ~Zig Ziglar*

## Fiori di Zucca

*Italians typically grow zucchini in their home gardens. The female zucchini flowers have the zucchini attached, so we don't touch those and let the zucchini mature to perfection on the plant. The male zucchini flowers are the ones with no zucchini attached, so we pick and fry the flowers in a sweet batter. Here is an old Italian family recipe, veganized and rendered gluten-friendly with a combination of spelt and kamut flour!*

**Ingredients:**
*Makes 6 to 8 flat dumpling-like servings*

½ cup (125 ml) kamut flour
½ cup (125 ml) spelt flour
¾ cup (180 ml) water
2 tablespoons (30 ml) raw cane sugar
½ teaspoon (2.5 ml) Himalayan salt
3 teaspoons (15 ml) egg replacer
½ cup (125 ml) grapeseed oil
Zucchini flowers, whole or shredded, stem and stamen removed

**Method:**
1. To prepare the batter, mix all ingredients, except the flowers, with a spatula in a large bowl.
2. If you have many zucchini flowers, you can dip the whole flower into the batter and fry it. If you have only one or two flowers, shred them and mix them into the batter. Some people prefer to discard the stem and stamen of the flower, as I suggest in this recipe.
3. Heat oil over medium to high heat in a frying pan.
4. Drop a large spoonful of batter or whole dipped flower into the frying pan. Fry for 1 to 2 minutes and flip over. They should be golden on each side.
5. Remove from oil and allow excess oil to drain on paper towels. Place on a serving dish and sprinkle with extra cane sugar if desired. Serve immediately.

# Lemon Poppy Seed Loaf

*The lemon zest is so delightful in this recipe, and the poppy seeds make a lovely companion to the lemon.*

**Ingredients:**
*Makes one loaf*

Dry ingredients:
2 cups (500 ml) whole wheat pastry flour
4 teaspoons (20 ml) egg replacer
2 teaspoons (10 ml) baking powder
1 teaspoon (5 ml) baking soda
⅓ cup (80 ml) raw cane sugar
2 tablespoons (30 ml) poppy seeds

Wet ingredients:
½ cup (125 ml) unsweetened almond milk (store-bought or see page 119 for homemade recipe)
⅓ cup (80 ml) kosher maple syrup
Juice and zest from one lemon
½ cup (125 ml) grapeseed oil
¼ cup (60 ml) water
Coconut oil to line baking dish

**Method:**
1. Preheat oven to 350°F (180°C).
2. Combine all dry ingredients in large bowl.
3. In another bowl, combine all wet ingredients.
4. Pour wet ingredients into bowl with dry ingredients and mix well.
5. Use rectangular glass or porcelain baking dish for cooking. Rub coconut oil onto dish to prevent loaf from sticking, or line baking dish with parchment paper. Pour mixture into dish.
6. Bake for 35 to 40 minutes, or until toothpick test comes out dry. Allow at least one hour to cool before slicing.

*"Don't gain the world and lose your soul. Wisdom is better than silver or gold." ~Bob Marley*

## Crazy-Crispy Kale Chips

*As crispy and savory as the potato variety we know and love, without the guilt! Indulge! Try not to eat them all before they go into the oven! If you have a dehydrator, you can dehydrate these chips instead of baking.*

**Ingredients:**
*Makes approximately 2 servings*

Bunch of raw curly kale, washed and patted dry with paper towels
1 clove of garlic, minced
1 to 2 tablespoons (15-30 ml) wheat-free tamari
2 tablespoons (30 ml) grapeseed or olive oil
2 tablespoons (30 ml) hemp seeds

**Method:**
1. Preheat oven to 300°F (160°C).
2. With your hands or a knife, cut away the spine from each kale leaf and discard. Cut the leaves into large chip-sized pieces. Make sure kale is thoroughly dry.
3. In a small bowl, whisk all dressing ingredients together (garlic, tamari, oil and hemp seeds).
4. Place kale in a large bowl. Pour dressing over the kale. With your fingers, rub each piece of kale with the dressing to make sure the pieces are coated evenly.
5. Cover large baking sheet with parchment paper and line up the pieces of kale in a single layer.
6. Bake for 20 to 25 minutes or until crispy. Flip pieces of kale over after 10 minutes.

## Banana Walnut Chocolate Chunk Cake

*It's no secret: I really love bananas! I love everything about bananas, and everything we can do with bananas, like make moist, rich cake. Very ripe bananas are necessary for this recipe, so if your bananas are not brown, wait a few more days before making this recipe. I enhanced the richness by added chocolate chunks. Pure comfort - try it! You can choose gluten-free flour for this recipe if you desire.*

**Ingredients:**

Dry ingredients:
2 cups (500 ml) whole wheat pastry flour
4 teaspoons (20 ml) egg replacer
2 teaspoons (10 ml) baking powder
1 teaspoon (5 ml) baking soda
⅓ cup (80 ml) dairy-free chocolate chunks
¼ cup (60 ml) walnuts, chopped

Wet ingredients:
⅓ cup (80 ml) kosher maple syrup
¾ cup (180 ml) coconut water
⅓ cup (80 ml) grapeseed oil

3 very ripe bananas, mashed
1 teaspoon (5 ml) vanilla extract
Coconut oil to coat the baking pan

**Method:**
1. Preheat oven to 350°F (180°C).
2. Combine all dry ingredients in a large bowl. Mix thoroughly.
3. Combine wet ingredients in separate bowl, including mashed bananas.
4. Pour wet ingredients into dry mixture and stir with a spatula.
5. Rub a small amount of coconut oil onto glass or porcelain baking pan. Pour mixture into pan.
6. If desired, sprinkle some chopped walnuts on top and add a few slices of banana.
7. Bake for 35 minutes or until toothpick test comes out dry. Allow at least 2 hours to cool before slicing.

**"The way to love anything is to realize that it may be lost." ~Gilbert K. Chesterton**

## Matcha Green Tea Pistachio Ice Cream

*Since Matcha tea comes in powdered form, it is perfect to add to ice creams or smoothies. A beautifully vibrant green color, Matcha tea is full of flavor and adds all the health benefits of a green tea to this non-dairy iced treat. Staying with the green theme, I added pistachios for the delicious flavor they add to ice cream. Not only is this recipe vegan, it's also sugar free! The ripe bananas add all the sweetness we need. This recipe does not require an ice cream maker machine.*

### Ingredients:
*Makes approximately 4 to 5 servings*

4 bananas, very ripe, chopped into chunks and frozen
1 cup (250 ml) unsweetened almond milk (store-bought or see page 119 for homemade recipe) or coconut milk
¼ cup (60 ml) raw pistachios, more for topping
1 tablespoon (15 ml) Imperial Matcha Ceremonial Green Tea

### Method:
1. Remove bananas from the freezer and blend all ingredients in a blender.
2. Your mixture may be too soft and more like a smoothie at this point. If so, place your ice cream in a large glass container and put it in the freezer for at least 2 hours. Once firm, remove from the freezer. Use an ice cream scooper to scoop out ice cream and place it into your serving cups. Sprinkle a few pistachios over top, if desired. Serve immediately.

## Jennifer's Comforting Apple Crumble Cake

*I've made this cake many times and people just adore it, especially my friend Jennifer, so I named it in her honor! A cross between an apple crumble and a cake, with a divinely delicious apple and cinnamon filling, it's so good you'll be begging for a second piece!*

**Ingredients:**

**Filling:**
8 large, sweet red apples, peeled and chopped into small pieces
1 cup (250 ml) unsweetened apple sauce
1 teaspoon (5 ml) ground cinnamon
⅓ cup (80 ml) raw agave nectar
1 teaspoon (5 ml) coconut oil
1 tablespoon (15 ml) lemon juice
½ teaspoon (2.5 ml) Himalayan salt
1 teaspoon (5 ml) vanilla extract

**Cake:**
Dry ingredients:
4 cups (1 L) whole wheat pastry flour or spelt flour
1 cup (250 ml) raw cane sugar
3 teaspoons (15 ml) baking powder
4 teaspoons (20 ml) egg replacer
½ teaspoon (2.5 ml) Himalayan salt

Wet ingredients:
1 cup (250 ml) grapeseed oil
¾ cup (180 ml) water
¼ cup (60 ml) unsweetened apple sauce

**Topping:**
½ cup (125 ml) almond flour
½ cup (125 ml) raw cane sugar

¾ cup (180 ml) old fashioned rolled oats
1 tablespoon (15 ml) vegan butter

**Method:**
1. In a large pot, combine all filling ingredients and simmer on low heat for 45 minutes. Set aside and let cool thoroughly.
2. Preheat oven to 350°F (180°C).
3. Combine all dry cake ingredients in a large bowl.
4. Combine all wet cake ingredients in a small bowl. Pour into dry ingredients.
5. Knead mixture into a firm loaf. If loaf crumbles or is too hard to work, add a tiny amount of water. Remove ⅓ of the mixture and set aside.
6. Press down remaining mixture in a glass or ceramic baking dish. Pour in cooled apple filling.
7. With remaining cake mixture, take small amounts and make palm-sized patches with your hands. Place patch by patch over fruit filling until all the fruit is completely covered.
8. In a small bowl, combine all topping ingredients. Rub mixture between fingers until it begins to form small clumps. Sprinkle topping over top of the cake.
9. Bake for 50 minutes. Remove from oven and let cool for at least 1 ½ to 2 hours before slicing. Serve on its own or accompanied with vegan coconut vanilla ice cream.

*"The animals of the world exist for their own reasons. They were not made for humans any more than black people were made for white, or women created for men." ~Alice Walker*

## Bliss Balance Brownie Balls

*Raw, vegan and gluten-free, I created these brownie balls with ingredients for each of our chakras. Have one and experience the bliss of balanced chakras!*

### Ingredients:
Makes approximately 20 to 25 brownie balls

½ cup (125 ml) raw walnuts, chopped
½ cup (125 ml) raw Brazil nuts, chopped
¼ cup (60 ml) ground flaxseed
1 small carrot, shredded
1 teaspoon (5 ml) fresh ginger, minced
¼ cup (60 ml) water
12 fresh dates, pitted and chopped
1 cup (250 ml) cacao powder
½ cup (125 ml) almond flour
1 cup (250 ml) unsweetened shredded coconut flakes
1 tablespoon (15 ml) coconut oil
½ teaspoon (2.5 ml) cardamom
½ teaspoon (2.5 ml) nutmeg
¼ teaspoon (1.25 ml) cayenne pepper
1 tablespoon (15 ml) cacao nibs
5 to 8 drops liquid stevia

### Method:
1. In a food processor, blend walnuts, Brazil nuts and flaxseed until powdery texture is achieved.
2. Add carrot, ginger and water to the food processor and continue blending until mixture starts to look smooth and sticky.
3. Add dates, cacao powder and coconut oil and blend. If mixture is too hard, add a tiny amount of water.
4. Transfer mixture to a large bowl. Add spices, cacao nibs, stevia and almond flour. Mix thoroughly with a spatula. Mixture will be very sticky.
5. Place mixture in the refrigerator for about an hour to harden and make it more manageable.
6. Remove from fridge. Using the palm of your hand, form small, round brownie balls.
7. Coat brownie balls with coconut flakes. Refrigerate in glass container for 2 to 3 hours to harden. Serve.

## Strawberry Shortcake Cupcakes

*The delightful taste of shortcake, but in a cupcake format, this recipe is a lovely treat for any party. Kids especially love this recipe!*

**Ingredients:**
*Makes 18 cupcakes*

1 ½ cups (375 ml) vanilla brown rice milk
2 teaspoons (10 ml) apple cider vinegar
2 ½ cups (625 ml) unbleached white flour
1 ½ cups (375 ml) raw cane sugar
1 ½ teaspoons (7.5 ml) baking powder
1 teaspoon (5 ml) baking soda
½ teaspoon (2.5 ml) Himalayan salt
¾ cup (180 ml) grapeseed oil
4 teaspoons (20 ml) vanilla extract

**Frosting:**
2 strawberries, thoroughly mashed
1 cup (250 ml) vegan butter
2 cups (500 ml) icing sugar

1 tablespoon (15 ml) vanilla extract
1 tablespoon (15 ml) water
Additional chopped strawberries for topping

**Method:**
1. Preheat oven to 350°F (180°C). Line muffin pan with parchment paper liners.
2. In a small bowl, mix rice milk and cider vinegar and set aside for 5 minutes.
3. In a separate bowl, mix flour, sugar, baking powder, baking soda and salt.
4. Into the small bowl with rice milk, stir in oil and vanilla extract.
5. Add wet ingredients to dry ingredients and mix until blended.
6. Spoon into muffin cups.
7. Bake for 25 minutes or until toothpick inserted into the center of the cupcake comes out dry. Let muffins cool thoroughly before applying frosting. You can refrigerate the cupcakes for a while before adding the frosting.
8. For the frosting, combine all frosting ingredients in a bowl and use a handheld mixer to whip mixture until smooth and creamy.
9. Use a pastry bag fitted with a star tip to apply frosting on the cupcakes.
10. Refrigerate cupcakes for about an hour to let the icing harden a little. Apply a piece of strawberry on each cupcake before serving.

*"To become wholly compassionate requires us to open our eyes and hearts, to behold the pain and exploitation our culture obscures, to arouse deadened emotions, and to rise above our egos."*
*~Joanne Stepaniak*

## AmoreTella Chocolate Spread

*Indulge your senses in this creamy, decadent chocolate spread. Also makes a perfect icing for many desserts.*

**Ingredients:**
*Makes approximately 3 cups*

1 ½ cups (375 mL) cacao powder
1 cup (250 ml) raw agave nectar
¾ cup (180 ml) vegan butter
⅓ cup (80 ml) raw or roasted hazelnuts
½ cup (125 ml) unsweetened hazelnut butter
4 teaspoons (20 ml) hazelnut oil
¼ cup (60 ml) unsweetened almond milk (store-bought or see page 119 for homemade recipe)

**Method:**
1. Blend all ingredients in food processor until smooth and creamy.
2. Serve on favorite bread, crackers, rice cakes or as an icing for desserts. Keep refrigerated.

## Cheese Scones

*When I say vegans don't have to sacrifice anything, I mean it – and this includes cheese! With the many vegan cheeses on the market and simple nut cheese recipes we can easily make at home, there is absolutely no need to deprive yourself. For this recipe, I created an irresistible dairy-free scone, a lovely accompaniment to a cup of tea or coffee. I use spelt or kamut flour since these are more "gluten-friendly" than wheat. The kamut flour makes slightly drier scones, whereas spelt makes them moister. If raisin cinnamon scones are more your fancy, an alternative recipe would be to include 1 cup of raisins (rather than cheese) and 1 teaspoon of cinnamon (rather than poppy seeds).*

**Ingredients:**
*Makes 8 scones*

Dry ingredients:
2 ¼ cups (560 ml) spelt or kamut flour, a little extra for work station
4 teaspoons (20 ml) egg replacer
4 teaspoons (20 ml) baking powder
1 tablespoon (15 ml) raw cane sugar
1 teaspoon (5 ml) Himalayan salt
2 tablespoons (30 ml) poppy seeds
1 cup (250 ml) vegan cheddar cheese, chopped into
small chunks

Wet ingredients:
½ cup (125 ml) grapeseed oil
1 cup (250 ml) organic plain soy milk

Vegan butter or coconut oil to line glass casserole dish

Method:
1. Preheat oven to 450°F (230°C).
2. In a large bowl, combine all dry ingredients, including ¾ cup (180 ml) of vegan cheese chunks and 1 tablespoon (15 ml) of poppy seeds.
3. In a small bowl, combine oil and soy milk.
4. Pour wet ingredients into dry ingredients and mix well.
5. Lightly dust work station with spelt flour. Knead dough on work station, sprinkling a little more flour if dough becomes too sticky.
6. Pat down into a circular shape.
7. Spread small amount of vegan butter or coconut oil in circular glass casserole dish to avoid sticking while baking.
8. Place circular shaped dough into glass casserole dish. Sprinkle small amount of flour over top and pat down.
9. Slice into 8 wedges. Place in the oven and bake for 15 minutes.
10. Remove from oven and sprinkle remaining cheese and poppy seeds over top. Return to the oven to bake for 5 more minutes, or until top is golden. Remove from oven and let cool briefly before slicing.

*"As we become purer channels for God's light, we develop an appetite for the sweetness that is possible in this world. A miracle worker is not geared toward fighting the world that is, but toward creating the world that could be." ~Marianne Williamson*

## Chocolate Raspberry Valentine Cake

*I created this chocolate raspberry treat as part of a Valentine's Day fundraiser for the Montreal SPCA and Mercy for Animals. It is always an honor to be involved in raising funds and spreading awareness for such important groups. This cake was a huge success! I have made it both ways, chocolate frosting or the raspberry coulis, and both are exquisite.*

**Ingredients:**
**Chocolate Cake**
1 ½ cups (375 ml) unbleached white flour
⅓ cup (80 ml) unsweetened cacao powder
½ teaspoon (2.5 ml) baking soda
½ teaspoon (2.5 ml) Himalayan salt
1 cup (250 ml) raw cane sugar
½ cup (125 ml) grapeseed oil
1 cup (250 ml) brewed coffee, chilled, or water
2 teaspoons (10 ml) vanilla extract
2 tablespoons (30 ml) apple cider vinegar
Coconut oil for baking dish

**Chocolate Raspberry Frosting**
2 ounces (57 grams) unsweetened dark chocolate
¼ cup (60 ml) fresh raspberries, mashed
3 tablespoons (45 ml) water
1 teaspoon (5 ml) vanilla extract
1 cup (250 ml) icing sugar

**Topping over frosting**
1 cup (250 ml) fresh raspberries
½ cup (125 ml) non-dairy chocolate chips

**Method:**
1. Preheat oven to 375°F (190°C). Spread coconut oil on baking dish to prevent sticking.
2. In a large bowl, mix flour, cacao, baking soda, salt and sugar. In another bowl, combine oil, coffee and vanilla. Pour liquid ingredients into the dry ingredients, and mix until smooth.
3. Add vinegar and stir briefly (the baking soda will begin to react with vinegar). Quickly pour batter into prepared pan.
4. Bake for 25 to 30 minutes. Allow cake to cool slightly before adding frosting, slicing or adding coulis.
5. To prepare the frosting, in a small saucepan, melt chocolate over low to medium heat. Once fully melted, remove from heat and stir in mashed raspberries, water and vanilla. Stir in icing sugar. Spread frosting on cooled cake.
6. Top frosting with whole raspberries and sprinkle non-dairy chocolate chips over cake.

Alternatively, top the cake with:

**Raspberry Coulis**
1 cup (250 ml) fresh raspberries
1 cup (250 ml) unsweetened raspberry jam

**Method:**
1. Blend raspberries and jam in a blender. Pour over each slice of chocolate cake before serving.

## Zucchini Cranberry Loaf

*The epitome of moistness and deliciousness, this zucchini loaf will definitely have you coming back for a second piece, and maybe even a third! This recipe works equally well with whole wheat pastry flour and spelt flour, or you may choose gluten-free options.*

**Ingredients:**
*Makes 2 loaves*

5 tablespoons (75 ml) ground flaxseed
½ cup (125 ml) water

Dry ingredients:
3 cups (750 ml) whole wheat pastry flour or spelt flour
1 teaspoon (5 ml) baking soda
2 teaspoons (10 ml) baking powder
½ cup (125 ml) raw cane sugar
1 teaspoon (5 ml) cinnamon
½ teaspoon (2.5 ml) nutmeg
¼ teaspoon (1.25 ml) Himalayan salt
½ cup (125 ml) raw walnuts, chopped
½ cup (125 ml) pumpkin seeds (optional)

**Wet ingredients:**
½ cup (125 ml) kosher maple syrup
1 teaspoon (5 ml) vanilla extract
½ cup (125 ml) water
¾ cup (180 ml) grapeseed oil
3 cups (750 ml) raw zucchini, grated (about 3 zucchini)
1 cup (250 ml) fresh cranberries

**Method:**
1. Preheat oven to 350°F (180°C).
2. In a small bowl, stir flaxseed and ½ cup (125 ml) of water and set aside for about 15-20 minutes to let thicken.
3. In a large bowl, combine all dry ingredients and spices: flour, baking powder and baking soda, sugar, cinnamon, nutmeg, salt and half the walnuts and pumpkin seeds (save the other half to sprinkle on top of the loaves).
4. In a small bowl, stir all wet ingredients: maple syrup, vanilla extract, water and grapeseed oil. Pour in flaxseed mixture.
5. Pour wet ingredients into dry ingredients and stir. Add zucchini and cranberries and mix well.
6. Line 2 rectangular glass casserole dishes with parchment paper to avoid excessive sticking. Pour batter into casserole dishes, half the amount in each to make 2 loaves.
7. Sprinkle remaining walnuts and pumpkin seeds on top of the loaves.
8. Bake for 55 minutes. Remove from the oven and let cool before slicing.

*"People look at me as a vegan and conclude that since I stepped on a snail or because the vegetables I eat resulted in a tractor death for a squirrel somewhere in Paraguay that somehow vegans are hypocrites, which of course they're not since perfection is an unattainable goal and is something to be driven towards, never actually achieved. The difference between you and the vegan standing next to you is that while you're both going to step on a bug tomorrow, they've decided to dedicate their lives to as little harm as possible, completely independent from what you do. So in no way does the protozoan life form they step on negate your responsibility for the lamb you're paying a stranger to cut tomorrow. And falling 1% short of an unattainable goal is really good when you're standing next to someone who won't even try." ~Shelley Williams*

## ABOUT THE AUTHOR

Former corporate lawyer, Maria Amore now feels she has found her true purpose in this life: vegan cooking. Driven by her desire to heal herself from a debilitating illness, Maria diligently researched nutrition and "went vegan" overnight based on what she learned about healthy eating and compassionate living. Her love of cooking exploded with her newfound plant-based way of life.

Inspired to inspire, Maria teaches a vegan cooking course at McGill University in Montreal, Canada. She also teaches workshops on vegan cooking and juicing/smoothies, and offers private in-home sessions. In addition, Maria is a coach to those wishing to transition to a vegan lifestyle.

Having been a devoted animal lover her whole life, Maria is an animal advocate, participating in fundraisers for animal causes and campaigning to spread the word about the many benefits of a vegan way of life. In addition, she rescues, fosters and finds families for abandoned animals.

*Maria Amore, BA, BCL, LLB, Certified Raw Vegan Chef and Raw Food Nutrition Educator*

When Maria submitted this manuscript for publication, she was preparing to attend Living Light Culinary Institute in California to study gourmet raw vegan cuisine and raw food nutrition.
Today, Maria is working on future publications and preparing to move to Mexico.

She is thrilled about the upcoming opening of her organic vegan and raw vegan bistro in San Jose del Cabo in Baja California Sur, Mexico.

When people say, "Be the change you wish to see in the world," she whole-heartedly responds, "I am."

She can be contacted at **withamore@gmail.com**.

Lightning Source UK Ltd.
Milton Keynes UK
UKOW06f1322270514

232376UK00009B/28/P

9 781491 813904